"The timing of *Build to Prosper* could not be more relevant for business owners and management teams today. Many of my clients have successfully navigated the recent economic downturn but have found themselves working very hard for little or no return. The principles shared in this book have resulted in a number of my clients either stabilizing their business or returning the business to the profitability it deserves. I have had the great pleasure of watching owners and management teams move from resisting the principles in this book to embracing them and reaping the benefits. I highly recommend this book for business owners and their management teams looking to improve the profitability of their business and lenders who would like to help their clients be more successful. For a number of my clients, this book was the lifeline they needed and a way for me to preserve a profitable lending relationship."

—Greg Carasik,
Executive Vice President, Director,
Marquette Business Credit

"Cam's Business Modeling Methodology is a proven action plan for helping owners discover and leverage their businesses' intellectual properties to transform their enterprises to increased profitability. Cam teaches owners to identify and break the patterns that hold them back and frees them to discover strengths, transform business models, and innovate their way to prosperity once again. His real life experiences of helping entrepreneurs are inspirational!"

—Daniel S. Conway,
Managing Director,
FocalPoint Partners LLC

"*Build to Prosper* is a must read for any business owner who wants to add value to his company through innovation. Cam identifies eight economic business theories that can lead to marginalization and trap value inside a company. He then takes you through his ten-step Business Modeling Methodology process that will restore profitability and unlock hidden intellectual properties inside a business. His explanation of the importance of innovation to grow value inside any business is insightful and fresh. *Build to Prosper* is a lifetime of business wisdom in an easy to read book."

—Clay Hightower,
Business Development Director,
Rotork Gears

"*Build to Prosper* is an essential handbook for any business owner who is looking to unlock intellectual properties, the keys to prosperity in their business. In my experience in sales/marketing with companies such as Coca-Cola and Bristol-Myers Squibb, the resources needed to take any business to the next level have always been within the business itself. This is exactly what Cam eloquently brings out in his book as he discusses intellectual property."

—Robert Fukui,
President,
High Point Marketing, Inc.

"I highly recommend this practical and comprehensive challenge to established ways of thinking and evaluation. Cam's great insight is evident, but his approach and explanations make his wisdom accessible. The use of real world cases puts over his ideas and principles with realism so that you can directly apply them to your own business or organization. Everyone could benefit from these lessons, combining a wealth of experience with applied innovative thinking."

—Ruth Whitaker,
Chief Executive,
United Kingdom, Mission Aviation Fellowship, UK

BUILD
to
PROSPER

October 4th, 2013
Dear Rick,

BUILD *to* PROSPER

Secrets for Sustained Profitability

We have experienced great business success together and you are a friend. May you continue to Prosper

Cameron J. McConnell

Cam

Brown Books Publishing Group
Dallas, Texas

Build to Prosper
Secrets for Sustained Profitability

Brown Books Publishing Group
16250 Knoll Trail Drive, Suite 205
Dallas, Texas 75248
www.BrownBooks.com
(972) 381-0009

A New Era in Publishing™

ISBN 978-1-61254-116-7
LCCN 2013945318

Printed in the United States
10 9 8 7 6 5 4 3 2 1

For more information or to contact the author, please go to www.BuildToProsperBook.com.

To Ginny Reid McConnell

In a way, *Build to Prosper* brought us together. When we met in London in October 2009, you had already read my draft of the book and commented positively on my insights and commitment to helping business owners. We walked for hours in Trafalgar Square.

Just before we met, on September 29, 2009, the Dow Jones Industrial Average had dropped 777.7 points in one day. Throughout the world, the effects of this financial collapse were just beginning to impact all of us. You and I discovered that we shared the faith that this turbulence would be weathered over time. Most important, we had common dreams and visions about a restructured world economy.

When we married on May 23, 2010, you became my true coauthor, in life as in this book. You have supported my dreams to bring innovation back to America and helped in innumerable ways to write and edit this book. I am truly blessed to have you as my bride and dedicate this book to you and our future together.

Contents

Foreword

I am the founding partner of Levene, Neale, Bender, Yoo & Brill L.L.P., one of the leading corporate restructuring law firms in the United States. Having been in the restructuring field for nearly forty years, I have been involved with or represented clients in almost every industry and type of business. Our engagements range from simple informal solutions to complex multinational restructurings under the supervision of the United States federal court system.

Build to Prosper by Cameron McConnell is a breath of fresh air for anyone in business. The book is an easy read, replete with common sense, and brings a fresh perspective whose genius may be its simplicity.

Over the years, I have worked with Cam on many occasions. His success rate in turnarounds and operational enhancement in building businesses is impressive. I have never had a client complain to me about any aspect of Cam's Business Building Methodology or his style. Cam encourages his clients to think freely and creatively. Although it is natural for members of management to feel threatened when being analyzed by a consultant, there have been no reports to me of friction or problems that could not be resolved. From personal observation, this in large part is due to Cam's outstanding people skills.

Professionally it is a pleasure working with Cam on projects, and his business building invariably is reliable and vetted. He meets his time commitments. His analyses are explained with backup as appropriate.

Build to Prosper is *not* a book about Cam's skills as an economist or professional. It is *not* a promotional work designed to attract consulting clients and other business. Rather Cam seeks to share his secrets and trusted ideas about the evolution of business and how to adapt to today's changing economic environment. This book sets out a methodology with examples that make Cam's points clear and easy to assimilate. A business is not just "bricks and mortar." Often the real value of the business is in the intangibles which he calls "intellectual properties."

Build to Prosper is bright, innovative, and a welcome reprise from reams of data produced by the financial press.

David W. Levene, Esq.
Los Angeles, California

Some may try and tell us that this is the end of an era. But what they overlook is that in America, every day is a new beginning, and every sunset is merely the latest milestone on a voyage that never ends. For this is the land that has never become but is always in the act of becoming.

—**President Ronald Reagan**,
Presidential Medal of Freedom ceremony, 1993

Introduction

Is your business becoming marginalized? "Marginalized" means the *process by which you have made great efforts to increase sales but your business still has declining profitability.* I am convinced you are doing everything in your power to save your business, but you haven't been able to identify what is causing the decline in profitability and what is preventing the dynamic growth that you once experienced.

Be assured you're in good company. Clayton Christensen, currently the world's most profound management thinker, has discovered that the economic theory relied on by capital investors, owners, management, and financial lenders twenty years ago to measure reasonable returns on investments is not providing meaningful measurements in many current situations. He believes that what was taught was the right answer in the right situation, but now we are in the wrong situation, and these theories no longer create the results that we expect.

Christensen's revelation should encourage you because it suggests that other economic theories may also not be relevant today. *Build to Prosper* provides firsthand knowledge that explains why your business may be marginalized—because you made the right decisions in the wrong situations. Different economic theories you have relied upon in the past are causing your business to become marginalized. Given my decades of experience as a CIO, Chief Innovations Officer, it encourages me that Christensen so willingly admits that as business circumstances have changed, business owners and those who invest in their businesses need to take caution with past economic theories that have been taught and then relied upon and are challenging our very economic model of capitalism.

Build to Prosper provides the substantive evidence validating the *pattern* of these economic theories that have not worked in hundreds of companies over the last thirty years, causing businesses to suffer marginalization. I am often called in by bankers gravely concerned that a business customer is not going to be able to meet its loan obligations. The hope is that by accepting our help the owner can stabilize and rebuild and reinvest in innovation in his or her business and thus restore a healthy relationship with the bank. The bankers who turn to me know that my Business Modeling Methodology (BMM) process works. Just recently we were developing a relationship with a new financial institution, and when I told them about this book, they sent it to five current clients whom they felt would be reluctant to seek help. The business owners found the advice in this book so valuable that they decided to retain us and are already substantially improving their profitability.

After working with more than three hundred business owners, I have discovered that an owner's ability or willingness to make changes—to reverse the path of his or her business from being marginalized—requires the owner to understand and agree that an eroding *pattern* exists. Many businesses can be turned around to obtain profitability. However, this accomplishment is short-lived because the *pattern* has not been reversed, and the process of marginalization continues.

Build to Prosper is designed to help business owners at all stages of their company's development. Owners of mature businesses will find the knowledge they need to regenerate their businesses and accomplish the goal of earning sustained pretax profits over a period of years. Owners of businesses in their early cycle will learn from mistakes others have made and know how to avoid becoming marginalized, giving them a greater assurance of being successful. Owners in the startup phase will see how to choose a preparatory strategy to build their businesses and price their products or services properly from the beginning.

The book is divided into five sections. The first section begins by helping you determine whether your business qualifies as being marginalized. Then I outline the *pattern* inherent in the eight economic theories you have relied on that actually combine to marginalize your business further. At this stage, you will realize that *neither the state of the economy nor your competitors are the interfering conditions marginalizing your business.* I follow with a short explanation of what really works in relation to these theories and will show you in later chapters how your business can recover from being marginalized and have a bright future as long as you are willing to restructure your business to earn 10 percent pretax profits on annualized sales.

The second section of the book provides you with my step-by-step BMM process to apply to your business that will uncover the relevant economic theories causing it to be marginalized and help you create an action plan to return your business to profitability.

The third and perhaps most important section of the book focuses on innovation. I present a new perspective for you to consider: *Even with your marginalized business, I believe significant valuable resources in your business still exist.* I call these resources *intellectual properties.* As we apply the BMM process to your business, the process itself discloses these resources, and the intellectual properties become the foundation of future growth for your business. They are the *seeds of your inheritance* for your business.

To illustrate how effective the BMM process has been for our clients, throughout the book I share real-world cases of businesses that returned to profitability after we assisted them in discovering the true reason for their unprofitability and the steps necessary to reignite the vision for their company. The common thread running through all of these examples is the business owner's willingness to change the marginalized business *pattern.* We identify the *pattern* and then discuss how to choose and implement a new, revolutionary strategy to build a better business.

Once an owner agrees to the conditions that are revealed in the *pattern,* the BMM process of recovery can begin. This solution is defined as follows: *An owner's business has returned to earning sustained pretax profits that are sufficient to provide investment capital for innovations to create new products/services that will benefit future generations.* In many of these real-world cases, you will read about business owners who discovered their intellectual properties and how the pretax profits of their business dramatically increased:

- ➢ An aeromotive company went from losing $15,000,000 a year to earning pretax profits of $10,000,000 a year.

- A cookie franchisor went from losing $12,000,000 a year to earning pretax profits of $8,000,000 a year.
- A residential home developer went from losing $7,500,000 a year to making $7,500,000 in pretax profits a year.
- An appliance retailer went from losing $4,000,000 to making $12,000,000 in pretax profits a year.
- A pizza company went from losing $9,000,000 to making more than $5,500,000 in pretax profits a year.

The bankers with whom I work can assure you that the BMM process I am now sharing with you in *Build to Prosper* is worth the equivalent of a $100,000 consulting fee. Just recently, a banker called me to say that he had tried to convince a prospective client that if he would accept my help, the bank would become the company's new lender, but the owner refused on the grounds that he didn't want to pay $100,000 for a phase one and then phase two type of action plan that would take a long time. I informed the banker that in situations like these, within a period of ten to fifteen business days and a few more additional meetings as the BMM process is applied, the owner would reach his desired goal for significantly less money. Now you can apply that same BMM process for the price of this book!

My goal in sharing the wisdom of my experience is to get you back in the saddle! In America we need to take back what we have given up to other parts of the world. We have given up profits and our businesses are being marginalized! Jobs have been given up to other parts of the world. Innovation around the globe is becoming what Clayton Christensen describes as *disruptive* innovations.

In the Innovation section of this book, I will teach you that your customers are the intellectual properties of your business. Your customers are the bridge to your future technological growth. Your customers trust you, they depend upon you, and they desire that you will be responsive in creating and bringing to market future products and services for them. The keys to open the heavens for new innovations for your business rest with your trusting relationship with your customers. They are the cornerstone of your business's future.

It is my hope that as your business returns to profitability and you start to invest in innovation through the advice in this book, I will have helped you contribute to the new business growth that the world so desperately needs, which will then promote a new marketplace to exchange goods and services and make our world a better home for future generations to come.

WHY IS YOUR BUSINESS MARGINALIZED?

— ONE —

Marginalization

There is nothing as difficult and as expensive, but also nothing as futile, as trying to keep a corpse from stinking.

—Peter Drucker,
The Daily Drucker

When the business you own has not met the financial covenants of your loan agreement, have you been asked by your lender if you need help to fix your business so it can earn sufficient profits and return to conformity with the loan agreement covenants? If so, you probably remember your first reaction: How could a business advisor—in my case I am a CIO, a Chief Innovation Officer, but we will stick with business advisor as we proceed—help me with my business problems? Possibly your lender encouraged you to ask for help, and if you declined, the lender then suggested that you might start to look for a new lender. At that juncture, you probably decided to interview business advisors.

Even if your lender has not yet held this conversation with you, the likelihood is that your business is becoming marginalized. By marginalized, I'm referring to the *process by which you have made great efforts to increase your sales but your business still has declining profitability.* Despite everything you have done to save your business, you still haven't been able to identify what is interfering with the profitable growth that you once experienced. The key question is how much longer you are going to watch your business continue this process of marginalization.

I have dedicated thirty years of my career to helping business owners like you who are desperately seeking to return their enterprises to sustained profitability. As a prospective client, the first question that you would ask me is, "What do you know about my business?" In many cases, you either founded the company or purchased the business, or a family member started the business years ago and now you are the chief executive officer with decades of involvement in its management. Why in the world would you need my help?

In my experience, one of the most difficult things for a business owner to admit is that he or she needs help. The greatest hurdle to turning around a marginalized business is getting the business owner to become willing to accept help from me, a business advisor. Quite honestly, at this stage business owners like you are in denial that they need help, but this is a normal response. Coming to grips with the reality that your business is being marginalized and you need help is a *threshold* experience.

The best way to begin to address the problem is to ask yourself some tough, incisive questions to determine if your business has reached the point of needing help. If I were sitting in front of you in your office, after some preliminaries I would ask you to tell me about your business. Following that, I would ask you if you are no longer meeting your loan covenants and if so why *you* think you are unable to meet your loan covenants. Depending on the information you've given me, I usually ask some questions to help you pinpoint the reasons you believe your business is in trouble and then ask if you feel you need or want help. Most owners say no.

I then spend no more than ten minutes summarizing how we have been able to help owners, the methodology we use, and the time period it would take to see results. Most are stunned when I assure them that we can solve their problem within weeks, not months. That's when our conversation really takes off.

Now I am going to invite you to spend a few minutes asking yourself if any of the following symptoms or conditions exist in your business. Check any and all appropriate to your current situation:

Goal Setting and Business Plans

- ❑ Do you have a profitability goal or a return on investments goal?
- ❑ Is your business unable to perform to your continually revised business plans?

Business Policy, Systems, and Procedures

- ❑ Have you and your management team taken salary reductions?
- ❑ Have you and your management team foregone bonuses?
- ❑ Have you discontinued annual reviews and raises for your workforce?
- ❑ Have you curtailed workforce training and development programs?
- ❑ Do you have quality standards and procedures that are not being followed?
- ❑ Are your employees required to cover job responsibilities for terminated employees?

Marketing and Sales

- ❑ Are your sales declining and market share eroding?
- ❑ Are marketing and selling costs increasing as sales volume is declining?
- ❑ Are sales returns increasing?
- ❑ Are warranty claims increasing?
- ❑ Are customer complaints not being resolved?
- ❑ Are you following your company's pricing guidelines?

Financial Performance

- ❑ Has your shareholder equity diminished?
- ❑ Is your monthly operating performance resulting in pretax losses?
- ❑ Do you have unallocated manufacturing overhead?
- ❑ Is cost of goods manufactured increasing?
- ❑ Are your customers not paying you on time?
- ❑ Is more and more inventory becoming slow-moving?
- ❑ Are you not paying your venders on time, causing reduced credit terms?
- ❑ Are you in default of your loan agreement?
- ❑ Are you negotiating for or working within the terms of a forbearance agreement with your lender?

Personal

- ❑ Has your family lifestyle changed due to problems in your business?
- ❑ Are you losing your resolve to continue the leadership of your business?
- ❑ Are your family/management team members having difficulties adjusting to the changing business conditions?
- ❑ Are you being criticized by family members for losing their inheritance?

Estate Planning/Expanding Business Growth for Future Generations of Your Family

- ❑ Have you lost the vision for growth of your business?
- ❑ Is your business no longer investing in innovation by creating new products and services for your customers?
- ❑ Are you no longer giving dividends to family business owners?
- ❑ Are you no longer investing in your community?

Hopefully asking these questions has prompted you to reconsider whether your business needs help. I'll assume you have concluded yes! Now the question in your mind is whether I have the necessary experience and expertise to help you and whether my BMM process can return your business to profitability, Below is a short history of how I came to develop and utilize the method so successfully.

Can You Trust the BMM Process to Restore Sustained Profitability to Your Business?

My business building experience (business advising) started with business owners in the late 1970s. My credentials as a business advisor were first honed over thirteen years in the corporate world. Starting in 1966, I worked full time for two years at IBM while earning my bachelor of science degree in accounting. I learned valuable lessons about how IBM created products and services and developed channels of distribution to deliver these products on time to trusting customers throughout the world—lessons you will discover later in this book that are key to new profits through innovation.

When I completed my degree, I was hired by KPMG, an international accounting firm. Within a short period of time, I became a CPA specializing in international banking for KPMG's bank clients on the west coast of the United States. After I had worked at KPMG for five years, a major bank recruited me to oversee its foreign banking operations in New York, London, and Brussels, Belgium. These banks performed foreign currency trading throughout the world to hedge the loan commitments made to international corporations.

Following that, I was recruited by a Fortune 500 corporation and shortly thereafter became its director of mergers and acquisitions. This is where I began to master my business advising skills. The corporation owned approximately sixty diversified businesses throughout the world and sent me to visit these separate subsidiaries and assess the feasibility of each management team's growth plans, as supported by their semiannual business plans.

Where on earth would I begin? To start, I believed that a standard performance measurement was required in order to accurately compare these businesses. Corporate management and I agreed to use the measurement of return on investment. Once this measurement was applied, we found that a majority of the businesses missed the minimum expected threshold, yet they continued to request additional capital to invest in innovations that they expected would result in new, profitable sales. We discovered that after each six-month period, the management teams of these businesses would present their performance to us, and at least 80 percent of them had spent their capital for investments. Some may have accomplished increased sales, but all their pretax profits declined in relation to their revenue and capital invested.

We needed to find out what was causing this *pattern*. With that goal in mind, I created and implemented a BMM process in the hope that this analytical process would reveal the *pattern* behind these lagging pretax profits. Once we discovered the cause of this *pattern*, we would have to figure out a way to stop the erosion and, most important, determine what we would do differently to rebuild reliable, sustainable business results that maintain a reasonable pretax profit, creating sufficient capital to be invested in innovations, repeatedly, every six months.

As a first step, the corporation's board of directors agreed to a new profit performance measurement of earning a 10 percent pretax profit return on annualized sales. (We adjusted this goal for a few subsidiaries.) We began our work with several subsidiary management teams simultaneously and soon discovered the same *pattern*: *Management teams had all applied the same economic theories that they believed were appropriate to base their business decisions upon*. We then continued implementing the BMM process with these subsidiaries so the problems causing these unprofitable operating results could be uncovered. Once the process to uncover these results was completed, the management teams could see that their decisions were not achieving the results they expected. Action plans had to be developed to implement immediate changes to accomplish their expected goal of earning 10 percent pretax profits on annualized sales.

As the new approach to earn 10 percent pretax profit on annualized sales was being integrated throughout these subsidiaries, the corporation promoted me to a divisional chief executive officer responsible for heading up the management team of the largest aeromotive corporation in the world that repaired and overhauled jet engines for airlines across the globe. The Boeing 747 jumbo jet had been released a few years earlier, but just before my tenure began, the oil embargo had forced airlines around the world to ground their jumbo jet fleets due to escalated fuel costs. Sales and profits of the aeromotive company had dropped by at least 30 percent, causing the holding company's stock on the New York Stock Exchange to plummet to $7 a share.

As the new chief executive officer of this aeromotive company, I asked the holding company's management for permission to apply the BMM process. However, the team was convinced that the aeromotive company should declare bankruptcy due to the pretax loss that would soon be recorded for the fiscal year ending that exceeded $15,000,000 with almost $100,000,000 in annual sales (figures are in 1976 dollars). Management at the holding company was convinced that, given the current global economic crisis, there was no possible alternative. I persisted, asking management to trust me and try this analytical part of the BMM process. At last they agreed.

Once deployed, the BMM process revealed the creation of schedules, documents, and financial information that measured the detail of unprofitable past sales. These measurements helped my aeromotive management team clearly see the results of their previous thinking that rested on economic theories they had been taught in school that were correct in the past. Their thinking was the foundation of the *pattern.* Once they understood that these theories did not work in the present circumstances, we could go about making changes to improve the profitability of the business. The cornerstone of our work was to improve customer profitability.

With this goal in mind, we created a plan with specific action items to be implemented in order to return the business to profitability. As we worked through this process, my aeromotive management team gradually became believers that *the state of the global economy (the oil embargo) was not the interfering condition that marginalized the business.* The BMM process had clearly revealed to them that customer pricing index formulas and calculations of standard costing for products and services required adjustment. This process of making improvements continued for a few months, and immediately the business became profitable, eventually earning $10,000,000 in pretax profit. The monthly profits grew each month for the following two years. The success was so significant that it enabled the holding company's management team to implement a management buyout at forty-nine ~~cents~~ dollars per share.

As a consequence of leading the sustained recovery of this aeromotive business, that year I was chosen as the Young Executive of the Year in Los Angeles. However, I decided not to join management in its private ownership of the holding company assets. I had so much enjoyed working with the aeromotive management team in the rebuilding process that I believed my future was to continue working with business owners and their management teams, so I founded my own business advising firm.

Since 1979, our firm has served hundreds of clients. These clients have been privately owned and in some cases were referred by banks and financial institutions in the belief that we could help these business owners improve their profitability so they could return to the bank's performing asset portfolio and no longer be in default of their loan agreement covenants.

My hope is that the wisdom of experience offered in this book can help you return your business to sustained pretax profits to be reinvested in innovations. Before we continue, however, we need to discuss something else you're probably thinking about—the issue of trust. Can you trust that together we can make decisions in your business's best interest and not just to satisfy your bank, your lender's concerns, or any other third-party concerns? Often business owners fear that business advisors like me are also spies for the bank, with only the bank's best interest at heart.

Let me address that issue head-on. Early on in the process of rebuilding your business, your lender is hoping that you will cut as many costs as soon as possible. There have been times that our BMM process has been questioned by lenders in the initial phase of implementation. To the lender it appeared that we were not cutting costs deep enough.

The reason the lender may think this way is that our methodology is focused on *preserving the intellectual properties in your business so these resources may be used to build upon for your future innovation opportunities.* It is relatively easy to reduce your workforce and cut costs. However, your business will not have the time or money to rebuild your intellectual properties if they become compromised. As the methodology is applied, your company's valuable intellectual properties will be discovered. Once you become aware of these key resources, rebuilding your business takes on a whole new meaning and purpose.

When it comes to questioning the amount of cost cutting, I've been in your shoes. The first time I was ever questioned about my willingness to cut the workforce and expenses as a business leader was when I was working at the aeromotive company. The holding company was not only the owner but also the lender. Even as I was working with management to restore the business to profitability, the holding company had a preference toward liquidation of the business if it did not see quick results. To the holding company, this meant that results were to be measured by immediate, drastic cuts in staff and expenses. The owners believed that our cost reductions should include the elimination of the management information systems (MIS) operation and the jumbo jet engineering department.

These reductions would have saved millions of dollars, but our analysis of the MIS and engineering operations disclosed that these resources were vital intellectual properties developed by the company over the past several years. We estimated that to try to recreate these intellectual properties would take years as well as tens of millions of dollars. We also assumed that a supporting professional workforce could be recreated. In our methodology action plan, we developed a database of maintenance requirements and costs for the jumbo jet engines from the FAA compliance documentation. We used this information to help manage the future requirements of engine time and expected depth of maintenance required as well as related costs for existing and future customers. We then provided business plans to the engineering and maintenance departments at airlines around the world to assist in managing their fleets. This technology became the foundation for future innovations, and as a consequence, we convinced the holding company not to shut down these departments.

I have related my professional history because it is vital that you trust me. You have been successful in developing trust with the customers you serve. My job is to earn your trust as we continue through this book. The following case should persuade you.

Case 1

The Owners Who Initially Said No

In this situation, both owners had concerns about the performance of their manufacturing and distribution business, and they knew changes were necessary. At the beginning of our engagement, the owners suggested that we short-cut our work because they knew the major decision that needed to be made for their business.

On the first day of the engagement, both owners expressed their belief that the channels of distribution for the business required restructuring. They knew that they currently could not meet their customers' overnight delivery expectations and believed that if they could make just these changes, their business could return to profitability. This restructuring would eliminate twelve regional sales managers who handled all contact with their major customers.

I discussed with the owners that overnight delivery was necessary to meet customer expectations. I suggested that we put this into a commitment for change in our action plan, and throughout our conversation the owners struggled with their loyalty to these twelve regional sales managers. That afternoon the owners told me that they could not be disloyal to their people. They did not want to make these changes, so I returned the retainer check they had given me that morning.

The following week the most unusual thing happened. The owners called and said that they wanted to proceed. They suggested that we apply the BMM process, hoping it might reveal a possible solution to saving some of the regional sales managers. When we started again the following week, we agreed to continue to resolve the restructuring of their channels of distribution.

The owners agreed to change their method of distribution to get their products to market. The existing salespeople were replaced and regional sales managers became managers of the distribution facilities. This strategy not only saved valuable customers but also became the foundation for creating new customers. The owners would in time learn the value of meeting customer needs for overnight delivery.

As a result of applying the BMM process, the company began to earn sustained profits exceeding 10 percent of sales over the next several years. This sustained growth eventually required additional capital. The owners were then able to access their accumulated retained earnings to obtain the primary resources needed to innovate—to rethink, rework, and retool their business to remain a leader in providing the products and services demanded by existing and new customers. The owners who initially said no changed their minds and were willing to apply the principles of the BMM process to build to prosper!

All of the cases like this one are from real clients. I hope that they will inspire you to have faith that the BMM process will bring success to your business as well. Success is to earn sufficient pretax profits for you to reinvest into future innovations as these business owners accomplished.

In the next chapter, you will discover your business *pattern*, the results of your decisions based on economic theories that may not be working in your business circumstances. Then, by applying the BMM process outlined in section 2, you and your management team will become skilled at how to develop a new business plan and implement action items that will return your business to earning pretax profits to invest in innovation that supplies your future customer needs. Let's get started!

—TWO—

Your Pattern: Economic Theories That No Longer Work

One of the top marketing lessons for the highly competitive twenty-first century—the most crucial one—is that buying customers doesn't work.

—Peter Drucker,
The Daily Drucker

I define the term *marginalized business* as the process by which you have made great efforts to increase your sales but your business still has declining profits. In order to understand why this is happening, we must first look at the foundational economic theories that you may have relied on when you started your business or that you have relied on in running a business that you inherited or bought.

The Eight Trusted Economic Theories

By now, you will no doubt agree that the economic theory that measures a business's performance by applying return on investment no longer works. This is the first economic theory that is part of your *pattern* that leads to marginalization. Below I summarize additional economic theories that you were taught and based your business decisions on that also contribute to the problem causing your business to suffer. You will notice that these economic theories are amazingly integrated and dependent on each other and for that reason contribute jointly to the problem:

- Reliance on expected return on investment to provide sufficient pretax profits
- Reliance on cost-led pricing of your products and services to provide adequate gross profits
- Reliance on break-even analysis to calculate reliable incremental profit contributions
- Reliance on incremental profit contribution after attaining a breakeven to justify price reductions
- Reliance on reducing prices after covering fixed and some semi variable costs of manufacturing to increase sales
- Reliance on product and service life cycles predetermined by break-even analysis

- ➢ Reliance on extended product and service life cycles based upon enhanced engineering and other product enhancements through innovation
- ➢ Reliance that your growth strategies extend the life cycle of your business

The Results of Economic Theories That No Longer Work

The eight economic theories I've just cited combine to marginalize your business. How do I know? My experience with hundreds of clients over the past thirty years has provided ample evidence. Let us briefly discuss these economic theories.

1. Return on Investment

   We have previously discussed return on investment, but let us look at an example of what has been taught. For our purposes, we will structure a business in which you have accumulated equity (investment) of $10,000,000. For the current year ended, you record sales of $100,000,000. Return on investment theory in the past has suggested that 10 percent pretax return on equity is a sufficient return. Therefore 10 percent in equity of $10,000,000 equates to $1,000,000. So the pretax profit goal expectation becomes $1,000,000.

2. Cost-Led Pricing

   When you apply cost-led pricing economic theory, you will mark up the costs of your products sufficiently to yield a pretax profit of 10 percent of equity. You then use these prices to prepare your break-even analysis.

3. Break-Even Analysis

   Business owners are taught that the key to managing their businesses rests on exceeding the break-even threshold of their businesses. Owners determine their fixed and variable product costs, add the expected pretax profit return, and then determine how many units they are required to sell to meet these expectations.

4. Incremental Profit Contribution—Pricing

   You were taught that incremental profits exist once your fixed and variable costs are covered. Owners decide to reduce overall selling prices because their fixed and a portion of their semivariable costs are covered, so they believe that there is room to reduce prices and try to keep existing customers.

5. Incremental Profit Contribution—Volume

   A business owner believes that once fixed and a portion of semivariable costs are absorbed he can reduce prices just to obtain new customers. Owners are not aware that these decisions regarding price reductions could have an effect on product life cycles.

6. Product Life Cycles—Break-Even Analysis
   To prepare your break-even analysis, you need to determine the life cycles of your products. Once you determined your product life cycles, you were able to allocate (depreciate, amortize) fixed costs over the product life cycle. This process of determining life cycles was quite interesting. First you had invested in innovations to make your products or services different so they could be distinguished in the marketplace. You had also thought through other economic theories regarding supply and demand. You determined the demand in the marketplace for your products or services as well as the possible competition. Once you had assured yourself of customer demand, you then estimated the product's useful life cycle. You also were quite confident that in the future you would develop new innovations.
7. Innovations to Extend Existing Product Life Cycles
   You knew that there would come a time when your products and services would have to be improved. As your business ages, you believe that you will

be able to create improved operating efficiencies. Economic theory teaches that you pass on these savings to your customers by reducing prices, thus protecting yourself from losing your customers to your competition. Also as time passes, you invest in short-term innovations that extend the life cycle of your products, and in my experience, you will usually reduce prices again. You become focused on product life cycles and ignore the *business* life cycle.

8. <u>Business Life Cycle</u>

   A business life cycle is shortened when you reduce prices to your customer, even with most product enhancements. Products will become commodities, and when this occurs, it means the life cycle of your business has been severely shortened.

As we discuss these economic theories, I know your mind is working overtime, thinking about the final possibility that your business life cycle may have been compromised. I realize that you are becoming very disappointed in these economic theories. You trusted them to help you build a profitable growing business, but now they no longer work.

You are not alone, however. In February 2013, Ron Johnson, CEO of J. C. Penney, told CNN that his reliance on the economic strategy of reducing prices and expecting increased volume as a result was not yet working. This validates Peter Drucker's insistence that of all the top marketing lessons for the highly competitive twenty-first century business, the most crucial one is that buying customers doesn't work.

The Lesson of J. C. Penney

The strategy employed by Ron Johnson when he was CEO of J. C. Penney was in stark contrast to that of the company's founder, James Cash Penney. Johnson was hired as CEO in 2011 to turn the company around. As the man who had provided the leadership behind Apple's retail marketing success, he had extraordinary credentials for the job. In relating my view of this situation, I hold no criticism in my heart toward Johnson or his board of directors, who are the finest assembled group of talent that investors in J. C. Penney can hope for.

As of the company's fiscal year ended February 28, 2013, however, J. C. Penney reported a record pretax loss of almost $1 billion. According to Ashley Lutz and Kim Bhasin at the CNBC *Business Insider* in early March, Johnson was running out of time to execute his strategy, which had been a disaster.

(In fact, Johnson was forced out of his position in early April 2013.) Lutz and Bhasin said that Johnson's turnaround strategy was largely centered on a new approach of fair and square pricing that claimed to offer the lowest prices daily. However, it appears that the public is not greatly interested in saving a little money on a purchase at the expense of top-notch customer service.

The reporters noted that James Cash Penney, who founded the company in 1902, built a great brand on superior customer service and suggested that Johnson should return to the company's roots. This is an excellent example to be aware of as we begin the BMM process section of the book. Once you complete this section, you will be equipped with the appropriate tools to apply to your marginalized business. These tools will then guide you to build your own action plan, which will rely on an assessment of your company's roots.

It is critical to understand these roots before you can develop an action plan to return your business to earning sustained pretax profits. I call these roots your company's *intellectual properties*. For J. C. Penney, those roots include customer loyalty, and at the end of this book, I present my analysis of what the next leader of J. C. Penney could consider changing to persuade loyal customers to return. After examining the eight economic theories we have just discussed, you may also have ideas that you think could help restore this great American company to profitability and customer loyalty.

Before we move on to the BMM process section of this book, I want to encourage you because you have also created significant values in your business. Most of these values have been in the background of your business. You cannot see pretax profits in these values; however, these values make up the future inheritance of your business. *The BMM process is designed to uncover the intellectual properties that are the solution to your business for future growth.* Just as the aeromotive business I worked for had created amazing value with its MIS and engineering departments for jumbo jets, your business has intellectual properties and valuable customers that will serve as building blocks to a prosperous future.

In addition to the first case I presented in chapter 1, this book includes other real cases of clients with whom I have worked over the years. Various economic theories that have not worked for these clients will be disclosed in these cases, which will help equip you with the knowledge necessary for you to understand your *pattern*. Once you understand your *pattern*, you will stop applying these economic theories to your decision making and develop your own action plan that will return your business to earning sustained pretax profits.

The next two chapters in this section of the book, Price-Led Costing vs. Cost-Led Pricing and Accelerated Decline of Life Cycles, expose the eight economic theories that no longer work in your business. You will see how these economic theories are the very root of your *pattern* that is causing your business to become marginalized.

— THREE —

Price-Led Costing vs. Cost-Led Pricing

Why is your business marginalized? Because you expected to earn an incremental profit by increasing your sales volume and by reducing your sale prices.

Now I will expose the core economic theories that get to the very root of your *pattern*. Most owners start their businesses by applying the economic theory of a break-even analysis. You prepared this analysis to determine how many products (units) had to be sold at a price sufficient to cover

1. All of your manufacturing costs
    - Direct manufacturing costs
    - Indirect manufacturing costs
    - Variable manufacturing costs
    - Fixed manufacturing costs
2. All of your marketing and selling costs
3. All of your general and administrative costs

Most importantly, you then tried to determine how many additional products needed to be sold to earn a pretax profit.

This break-even analysis is the foundation you relied on when you first applied the economic theory of earning incremental profits for your business. The owner determines his product prices by his costs and expected incremental profits. I need to mention again that, at best, an owner may establish his annual pretax profit goal on an expected percentage of his return on investment.

This process of determining your costs first to determine incremental profits is called *cost-led pricing*. Throughout the life of their businesses, most owners constantly struggle to determine what their customers are willing to pay. In this struggle, owners defer to cost-led pricing because this is the economic theory they learned when they prepared their first break-even analysis and started to determine what should be a reasonable incremental profit return on investment.

Instead the BMM process teaches owners that *price-led costing* should be used to determine the prices at which they will sell to customers. Drucker corroborates what the BMM process has been teaching for decades, namely that *price-led costing* should be applied to determine prices and costs. When business owners apply cost-led pricing for their products and services, they underprice their products and services!

To demonstrate the devastating results of basing your profit model on cost-led pricing, I will now share the stories of two different clients who applied this theory to their businesses. We will call the first one the Cookie Case, and the second the Appliance Case. I will briefly outline the initial circumstances of these two businesses when we started our engagement with them. Later in the book, I will reveal the results for these two owners after we applied the BMM process and based their model on *price-led costing.* You will learn that all of the owners in the cases I share in this book implemented *price-led costing* to accomplish the goal of earning 10 percent pretax profit on annualized sales.

The cookie company was a franchise with both franchisor-owned stores and franchisee-owned stores. These retail stores sold various types of cookies but predominantly chocolate chip cookies. The owner and his wife were famous. They developed great recipes for their cookies and designed a store footprint with state-of-the-art equipment to bake these cookies. Consumers fell in love with their cookies because of the recipes and baking process. Premier sites were leased for these retail outlets. The owners spared no expense on lease costs, personnel costs, equipment costs, and cookie ingredient costs to provide customers the best experience. The owners were true marketers, but they were not skilled in financing. The owners knew how to train owners and personnel to make great chocolate chip cookies. However, they relied on professionals to develop the economic model for their franchise company. These professionals used cost-led pricing when they developed their store model break-even analysis to determine how incremental profits should be earned.

We were initially contacted by a bank that referred us to a law firm representing the owners and their business. The law firm was hopeful we could help the company, which was experiencing substantial financial losses. They informed us that each retail store was losing money and that the franchising authorities in several states were going to require the franchisor to go dark, which meant that the franchise company would have to cease and desist from selling any future cookie retail stores in that state until certain conditions were met. The law firm told us that a Big Four CPA firm's management advisory specialist had suggested the franchisor consider liquidation. The hope of the law firm was that the BMM process could offer an immediate solution to return their client to earning sustainable pretax profits.

We worked quickly with the professionals the franchise company used to review their cost-led pricing methodology. The professionals disclosed how they created the financial model for a retail store. They used a break-even analysis to determine how many cookies a store had to sell to break even, and then they calculated how many more cookies were required to be sold to make an incremental profit. They used the investment in the store by the franchisor or the franchisee to determine a reasonable annual pretax profit return. They knew the volume of cookies to be sold, their costs, and an expected reasonable pretax return. Not one store was performing to their model. Nevertheless the professionals were convinced that their cost-led pricing theory was sound and the problem could be solved by increasing sales volume to increase the incremental profit. To accomplish this, they had a plan to hire salespeople to sell chocolate chip cookies for catered events.

The second example I want to use here to show the devastating results of cost-led pricing is the Appliance Case. This client was a regional retail appliance seller with six retail outlets. The company sold appliances including ovens, washers, dryers, refrigerators, and TVs. All of these products were extremely price sensitive due to the competitive prices in the marketplace and price-driven customers.

We were referred to this business by the owner's bank because all six retail outlets were losing money. In our initial discussion with the owner, he said that he had a great pricing strategy determined by break-even analysis that was structured to provide adequate pretax profits in the competitive marketplace that his business served. He invested heavily in advertising and promotions on regional TV. Although he admitted that he was taking money from his personal savings to keep the business running, he was convinced that his advertising and promotions would generate the necessary increased sales volume to earn incremental profits.

With these two case histories as background, we will proceed to the next chapter, Accelerated Decline of Life Cycles, where you will see the catch-22 you create in your business by applying cost-led pricing economic theory.

– FOUR –

Accelerated Decline of Life Cycles

You have just seen in the previous chapter how business owners have applied the economic theory of break-even analysis to determine their cost-led pricing. Owners believe that once their fixed costs are covered from existing sales that incremental profits will come from additional sales.

Now we will discuss more economic theories that owners rely on that do not work. Not only do business owners believe that incremental profits exist above the break-even threshold, but they also believe that due to this available incremental profit they can obtain more sales volume by reducing product prices for new customers and still earn additional pretax profits from the incremental profit that they believe exists. Consequently owners reduce prices to obtain increased sales volume.

I have provided a diagram of a simple product/service life cycle:

Chart 1

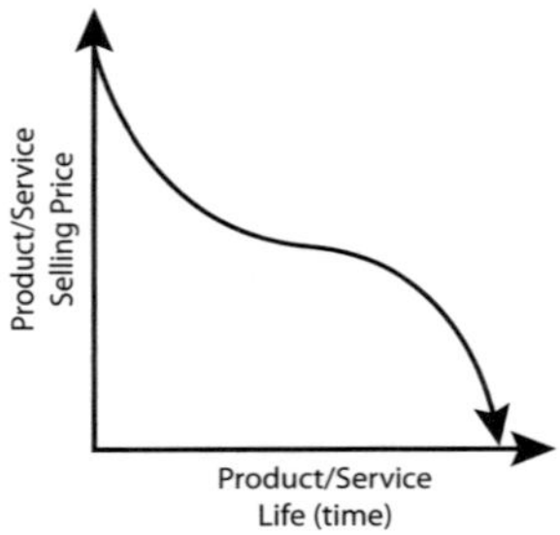

This diagram is very helpful for you to refer to during this discussion. When you started your business, you prepared a break-even analysis to determine your product/service life cycles. This determination was necessary so you could decide how to allocate fixed and variable costs over the expected life cycles of your products or services to determine your cost-led pricing.

Over time, however, demand for most products and services declines unless they are upgraded. Otherwise the life cycle for a product or service reaches a peak in customer demand, and then the demand will decline over time. Practically speaking, the product or service becomes a commodity until demand diminishes.

When a business becomes marginalized, most owners do not have any new products or services that they are planning to bring to market. They are trying to do the best with what they believe they have to work with at present. Under these marginalized conditions, due to the shortened product life cycles, they learn that their business life cycle has been shortened.

I will now share the case of a client to demonstrate how a business cycle can be compromised when an owner reduces prices to increase volume and how fast it can happen.

Case 2

The Client Who Was Kidnapped

This client was a food processor/distributor. The owner had a friend who had been a client of mine, and this friend referred me to the owner to help him return his business to earning sustained profits. Shortly after the owner engaged us, he revealed that the year before he had been kidnapped by several thieves who forced him to go back to his office, open his vault, and give them all his money. They then took his expensive watch and wedding ring, beat him, tied him up, left him in the office, and drove off in his car. The owner was not found until the following morning.

This traumatic experience had caused so much psychological damage to the owner that his business was almost beyond repair. The owner had stopped going to the plant, preferring instead to negotiate by phone with his customers on the terms and conditions for orders. As his business became increasingly marginalized, the owner had decided to try to increase sales volume by reducing sale prices.

Twelve months after the kidnapping, the business recorded a statement of operating loss of $5,500,000. This was the first year that the business had ever recorded a loss. After the owner communicated this loss to his secured asset-based lender, the lender asked the owner to find a new lender and pay off the loan.

To make matters worse, the CPA firm retained by the owner had just given him a draft of their opinion on the status of his financial statements. To his dismay, the CPA firm was qualifying their opinion of his business financial statements due to their concern regarding his business as a "going concern." The CPA firm told him that due to both the significant statement of operating loss of $5,500,000, and the fact that the owner did not have a secured asset-based lender with a future minimum twelve-month lending agreement in place, they could not express an opinion regarding his ability to remain in business.

In one year, this business owner had severely marginalized his business. He had not only shortened the business's product life cycles but also actually caused the business life cycle to be shortened to the point that he almost put the business to an end.

When I first began my engagement with the owner, he was very reluctant to go forward. He suggested that it was possible that his best choice was to liquidate his business. I asked him if he was familiar with the accomplishments that we obtained with his friend's business by applying the BMM process. He said yes. When I asked him if his friend had discussed the details of the BMM process with him, he said yes, that he knew his friend was still actively applying the BMM process to his business even after I had completed my engagement with him.

I then encouraged the owner to try to work with me and his CFO to create an action plan. I assured him that if he was not comfortable with the action plan that we built, then he could liquidate his business. The business owner agreed to proceed.

I knew that this business owner loved his business. He had spent more than twenty-five years successfully building it. I believed that the owner was so scared of being kidnapped again that he felt he had no other choice than to operate his business from home.

The owner used his own trucks to deliver to major franchise restaurants refrigerated foods that were processed and prepared for cooking. Until the last year, the quality and process of preparation by the business differentiated the owner's food products from the competition. Customers said his foods tasted the best when cooked in their kitchens and that the owner was the only one they could rely on to deliver these foods to them on a daily basis. His customers depended on just-in-time delivery, and in the past the business had met this goal.

I saw this as part of the answer to save the owner's business. However, we continued to complete our BMM process. When we came to the last step of the BMM process before developing an action plan, we prepared an inventory of the intellectual properties the owner had created in his business. The following intellectual properties became vital to saving the business:

- Trusting customers
- Loyal customers
- Best quality prepared foods
- Best-tasting foods when cooked
- Overnight delivery

Before I discussed with the owner how he could rebuild his business using these intellectual properties to develop his action plan, I asked him if he would be willing to relocate his business. He told me it was impossible! He said that even though he had to have three shifts because his plant capacity was less than adequate to support customer demands, his refrigeration capacity and design would cost too much to rebuild and relocate. I persisted, asking him where he would want to be located if he had the choice. He quickly named another nearby county that he viewed as safe to him as well as most desirous in terms of better distribution for his fleet of trucks in relationship to his customer base. I then asked him to call a real estate broker in that county and see if a refrigerated building was currently available. Within one week, the owner had found an ideal new plant available!

This owner now had hope that he could possibly return to his workplace if we could put together a plan to ensure it would earn sustained profitability. Once he was no longer a prisoner of fear, he was eager to complete his action plan.

As you might guess, this action plan included a commitment by the owner to move his plant. However it was the intellectual properties of the business that saved his company. The move alone saved the owner more than $5,000,000 in plant cost savings and reduced distribution costs. However, his business still was not profitable. The action plan required that the business owner meet privately with each major customer and discuss the following:

1. That he was returning to work full time to his newly relocated plant
2. That the new plant had greater capacity, an issue that had concerned his customers because their franchises were growing and they had been concerned that his former plant did not have enough capacity to meet their demand
3. That he could assure them of overnight delivery
4. That he needed to increase their prices by an average of 10 percent

To the owner's joy, his customers were more than willing to accept these price increases. They told him that they had accepted his previous price reductions as a sign that he was going out of business and that they needed time to find a new food processor/distributor vendor. The combination of cost savings and price increases helped this owner reach his profit improvement goal. Best of all, the owner had hope for the business that meant so much to him. He had his life back!

The ten preparation steps of the BMM process are discussed in latter chapters. Then in chapter 13, you will discover the core intellectual properties you have created in your business that you will be able to leverage to extend your business life cycle. You will then understand that you have a foundation to build upon to restore the life to your marginalized business. We then show you in chapter 14 how to develop your own action plan to make this a reality.

Let us now begin the actual BMM process.

THE BUSINESS MODELING METHODOLOGY (BMM) PROCESS

—FIVE—

Introducing the BMM Process: Goals

Welcome to this section of the book that outlines the BMM process. The goal of this process is to help you return your business to earning sustainable pretax profits. In chapter 1, we discussed the genesis of the BMM process. In this chapter, I briefly summarize the step-by-step process that targets the work you need to do to attain the ultimate goal of returning your business to earning sustainable pretax profits.

I believe that the condition of your bottom line today creates fear in your mind regarding the future viability of your business. When you are in fear, you cannot see. You become consumed with trying to *save* your business. You do not see that many policies, systems, and procedures in your business are causing this current feeling of fear.

Like many other business owners who have been highly successful in the past, you have relied upon the eight economic theories we discussed in chapter 2 to develop those policies, systems, and procedures that are no longer working. The BMM process will reveal what is not productive and will teach you corrective actions to eliminate nonproductive policies, systems, and procedures and replace them with sound business practices to return your business to earning sustained pretax profits.

Here are the ten steps involved in the BMM process:

Step 1: Preparation of previous twelve months' adjusted sales analysis

Step 2: Preparation of previous twelve months' adjusted marketing and selling expense analysis

Step 3: Preparation of previous twelve months' adjusted cost of goods sold analysis

Step 4: Preparation of production process analysis

Step 5: Preparation of previous twelve months' customer marginal profit contribution analysis

Step 6: Preparation of pricing analysis

Step 7: Preparation of previous twelve months' adjusted general and administrative expense analysis

Step 8: Preparation of previous twelve months' adjusted statement of operating profit or loss

Step 9: Preparation of profit improvement goal

Step 10: Preparation of inventory of your intellectual properties

All of these steps lead to the development of your action plan.

At first glance, this may sound like a lot of work. In my experience, you should be able to complete the BMM process within ten to fifteen business days. To demonstrate how worthwhile it can be to take the time to complete these steps, I will now share another case where we successfully applied the BMM process. As you read through it, make mental note of which procedures outlined above were utilized to solve the problem.

Case 3

The Owner Who Saved $3,000,000

This case involved a client who came to us in a most unorthodox manner. The client had just bought a manufacturing business from the seller. The terms of the purchase were

- 80 percent ownership
- Purchase price of $1,500,000 for the 80 percent ownership with no down payment required and equal monthly payments over the next 120 months, plus interest

- Stock pledged in case of default
- Seller to receive $8,000 a month consulting fee for five years
- Seller to receive a $1,500,000 life insurance policy on buyer in case of his death

The buyer believed that he would need approximately $3,000,000 to invest to build this business. We were referred to help him return the business to earning pretax profits that would be sufficient for him to borrow the $3,000,000.

The previous seller had a president who was still running and managing the business for the buyer. We applied the BMM process with the buyer, the company president, and their management team. The marginal product profitability schedule that we prepared for a month for this business looked like this:

Chart 2

Description	Product A Category	Product B Category	Service Category	TOTAL
Sales	$630,000	$376,000	$541,000	$1,547,000
Total Mfg Cost	($536,200)	($244,000)	($ 436,000)	($1,217,000)
Gross Margin	$93,800/ 15%	$132,000/ 35%	$105,000/ 19%	$330,000/ 21%
Marketing/Sales Costs	($65,000)	($42,000)	($55,000)	($162,000)
Marginal Product Profit Contribution	$28,800	$90,000	$50,000	$168,000
	4%	24%	9%	11%

The general and administrative expenses for a month were $152,000. The interest for one month was $50,000. So the statement of operating profit/loss in summary for a month looked like this:

Chart 3

Customer Marginal Profit Contribution	$168,000
Less General/Administrative Expenses	($152,000)
Less Interest	($50,000)
Monthly Pretax Loss	($34,000)
Annual Pretax Loss	($408,000)

The annual sales equaled $18,564,000.

Chart 3

Reasonable pretax profit should be 10 percent of sales	$1,856,400
Plus the recovery of the loss from the BMM process Statement of Operations	$408,000
The profit improvement goal became (for the following twelve months)	$2,264,400

During the preparation of the statement of operating profit/loss, the following was revealed:

- ➢ The company president had *no* experience as a CEO before he was hired.
- ➢ Based on standard costs for products/services, the company had a monthly negative variance of $192,000 of unallocated costs to specific product/service bills of materials.
- ➢ The business had *no* pricing guidelines.
- ➢ There was *no* pricing management.
- ➢ Management believed that *all* the negative monthly standard variance belonged to only one product category.
- ➢ Management believed that the material portion of the standard monthly variance was due to severe quality problems.

- ➢ The company president blamed the previous owner for making special price concessions with new customers to obtain increased volume.
- ➢ Ongoing negotiations with the unions revealed that labor costs were expected to increase by approximately 5 percent.
- ➢ An outside retired consultant was responsible for quality control.

From the information provided, you can see that our profit improvement goal was $2,264,000 (see chart 3). In this case, we also had to add $96,000 for the seller's consulting fee, and we included the principal to be paid to the seller for a year including interest, which was approximately $378,000. That brought the new profit improvement goal to $2,264,400 plus $96,000 plus $378,000 equal to $2,738,400.

As previously noted, the business had a negative monthly variance of $192,000 of costs not allocated to standard costs. Almost all of these variances had to do with poor quality control procedures, resulting in excessive labor inefficiencies and high scrap usage. The retired consultant responsible for quality control did not have a repair and maintenance program. The downtime of production equipment was using up 25 percent of the plant's daily efficiency capacity. The former business owner had tried to solve his operating variance problem by increasing sales volume and offering price concessions.

Based on this information, we developed an action plan (action plans will be explained in depth in chapter 14). Once we had completed implementation of the action plan, we had created more than 100 commitments for change that exceeded $4,000,000 through combined cost savings and price increases. More than $2,500,000 of these improvements came from reducing the costs to manufacture products over the next twelve months.

After the new owner saw the results of all we had accomplished, he realized that he did not need to borrow $3,000,000 for his business. As an owner, can you imagine needing to borrow $3,000,000 to cover possible operating losses and repairs and maintenance to equipment within ninety days of purchasing a business? Now, with this news, over the next twelve months your business will earn $3,750,000. This owner would have sustainable pretax profits and his own capital to invest in future innovations. As it turned out, within a year the owner acquired another company and merged it into his business. By the following year, the owner had doubled his sales volume and still maintained his 10 percent return on sales as a pretax profit goal.

Earlier I asked you to think about which economic theories the owner in this business had relied on. Possibly you found evidence in this case that disclosed various economic theories that did not work. Here are the economic theories that I found:

1. Incremental profit contribution—pricing and incremental profit contribution—volume. The previous owner made special price concessions with new customers to obtain increased volume.
2. Cost-led pricing. The previous owner had a monthly negative standard cost variance of $192,000.
3. Break-even analysis. Management believed that the negative standard cost variance applied to one product category business life cycle. The previous owner reduced the prices of his products.

How did your findings line up with mine?

You are becoming more familiar with the eight economic theories and their effects that marginalize your business. As we implement the BMM process steps in your business, your *pattern* will be revealed.

— SIX —

Revised Marketing and Selling Expenses

Preparation of Previous Twelve Months' Adjusted Sales Analysis (Step 1)
Preparation of Previous Twelve Months' Adjusted Marketing and Selling Expense Analysis (Step 2)

In this chapter, we will cover the first two BMM process steps. Step 1 is the preparation of a previous twelve-month adjusted sales analysis. The purpose of creating this analysis is to identify dependable sales that you believe you can rely on recurring in the next twelve months.

Preparation of Previous Twelve Months' Adjusted Sales Analysis

Determining the adjusted sales for the past twelve months is a highly analytical process. The owner, senior marketing and sales executives, and the CFO make up the team to accomplish this task. The work starts by preparing a sales analysis by month and by major product or service category.

Once this is done, you prepare an analysis of total sales by customer and total sales by product or service. In my experience, only 80 percent of sales are necessary to produce this analysis, and in most cases this percentage comprises the majority of major customers.

With this information in hand, you and your team have to determine, by customer, if that customer's business will recur over the following twelve months. Often the marketing and sales executives pull out a previous sales history to help. In some cases, a customer's sales have been declining over the past few years. You must then factor this erosion into expected customer sales.

In addition, each customer's product/service mix is very important for you to review. You will find that your customers are also changing the mix of products/services that they buy from you. You will notice a trend that key products/services that you believe are most favorably priced are no longer being purchased or are being purchased in smaller quantities. You may have lost a customer from the previous year. In this case, you remove their sales from your sales base. I often discover that during the previous year management has reduced the selling price to some of their major customers. If so, this requires adjustment to make the price decrease consistent throughout the year, by applicable customer. Often at the end of the previous twelve-month period, you also have credits that have not yet been processed for major customers. In that situation, you must also reduce the total sales and individual customer sales figures by the appropriate credit amounts.

At the aeromotive company I mentioned before, after we completed the previous twelve-month adjusted sales analysis, we ended up with 20 percent lower sales than the actual previous twelve months. For most clients, I find that 15 to 20 percent is the usual amount of reduction to sales that occurs when we apply the BMM process to the actual sales in the previous twelve months.

Obviously you will be disappointed when your sales reductions fall within this range. You will realize that your hurdle to recover from the marginalization in your business has taken a turn for the worse. Please don't be discouraged. Remember that you are becoming a student of the BMM process. Your expectation should continue to be that once you complete this process and create an action plan your business will return to earning sufficient pretax profits to provide you with adequate capital to invest in future innovations.

Preparation of Previous Twelve Months' Adjusted Marketing and Selling Expense Analysis

We are now going to move to step 2, preparation of your previous twelve months' adjusted marketing and selling expense analysis.

Now that the BMM process has made a significant reduction to your previous year sales, you will want to cut marketing and selling costs. By preparing this analysis, you will know how much to cut and what precisely to cut when you begin to prepare your action plan.

First we are interested in adjustments only to the previous twelve months for marketing and sales costs. These types of adjustments are costs that were only partial costs in the past twelve months but will continue into the next twelve months. Examples of these adjustments include

- ➢ Draws for salespeople who worked less than a full year
- ➢ Salaries for salespeople who worked less than a full year
- ➢ Sales commissions for the past twelve months that have not been accrued
- ➢ Partial marketing/advertising campaign costs that need to be annualized
- ➢ Additional costs for expected trade shows that were not attended in the previous twelve months

- ➢ Any new marketing media costs for commitments made for the next twelve months

All of these adjustments will increase the marketing and sales costs for the prior twelve-month period.

Second review your pricing guidelines now so the information will be available for further analysis in later steps of the BMM process. You have just determined the various categories of sales for each major customer. Now you take these customers and compare the prices they actually pay for products/services to your pricing guidelines.

Next we analyze the methodology that you use to determine your product/service prices.

Usually you based your prices on cost-led pricing. This means that you determine your costs and then add a markup.

Many business owners have been misled by this markup methodology. As an example, a business owner once told me that he had a 50 percent gross profit formula. He takes all the costs of manufacturing a product and increases them by 50 percent. So he would take his cost of $1,000 and increase it by 50 percent, which makes a selling price of $1,500. But to demonstrate the fallacy of this approach, we then divided his gross profit of $500 by $1,500 (the selling price) and his gross profit was actually 33 percent. Suffice to say, this owner was in shock! The owner had a commission plan that gave each salesperson a split of commissions for any price they could get from a customer for selling a product over the cost-led pricing guidelines. Consequently many salespeople were making commissions significantly greater than expected by the owner. They were selling products at a 50 percent gross profit, so they were getting an additional 50 percent of the 17 percent price increase over the 33 percent pricing guideline formula.

I have found that most business owners base their pricing guidelines on this theory of cost-led pricing. In step 6, preparation of pricing analysis, we will completely review cost-led pricing compared to price-led costing so you can fully understand how critical the difference is when it comes to your ability to sustain 10 percent pretax profits.

The BMM process will help you make changes in your business that usually save many of these key customers that you may be losing, so it is not yet time to determine cost savings in marketing and selling expenses.

We will now move on to step 3, preparation of previous twelve months' adjusted cost of goods sold analysis.

— SEVEN —

Revised Cost of Goods Sold

Preparation of Previous Twelve Months' Adjusted Cost of Goods Sold Analysis (Step 3)

Most companies have a process that establishes their *cost of goods sold* by creating for each product/service a *bill of material* with related standard costs. The total of each month's standard costs should always equal the *cost of goods sold*. Our goal in this step is to audit the accuracy of an owner's process that determines the company's monthly cost of goods sold. Why do we do this? We must know the accurate cost of producing goods and services and the cost to deliver them (freight) to the marketplace, consistent with the adjusted twelve-month sales.

As we discussed in chapter 6, we have created documentation of each customer's sales for the past twelve months by dollar amount and by product/service categories. We compared the customer's actual sales revenue to the company's pricing guidelines. Now we take the previous twelve months of monthly cost of goods sold and compare those to the standard costs for the customer's products or services sold.

In almost all cases, the standard costs do not equal the monthly cost of goods sold. Why is this? The most important reason is *capacity!* Most companies allocate cost of goods sold based on the theory that their manufacturing/service operation is functioning at 80 to 85 percent capacity. Consequently manufacturing overhead is allocated over the amount of products/services that will be produced within that production capacity of 80 to 85 percent.

When we perform our audit, though, we almost always find that for any month there are always fewer units produced or services provided than expected. We find that most companies are performing at well below 80 to 85 percent of operating capacity.

Our purpose is to determine accurate monthly cost of goods manufactured.

Case 4

Costs Greater Than Selling Price

Our client, a national printing company, had determined it could sell one hour of printing press time for $200.

The company had also computed the amount it would charge for labor, paper, ink, and prepress at standard hourly rates. However our example for this client is only for the hourly rate sold at $200 for one of its printing presses. After applying the BMM process, company officials discovered that their standard cost for this hour of printing time was actually $245 rather than the $145 they had previously determined. Their assumptions to determine these costs were based on the following factors:

Machine Use

- Useful life of the printing press
- Number of shifts for the press daily
- Number of printed sheets of paper per hour (printing press capacity)
- Downtime for paper changes
- Downtime for maintenance
- Downtime for shift changes
- Number of days worked in a week

Manufacturing Overhead

- Allocation of rent/building costs
- Allocation of utility costs
- Allocation of maintenance costs
- Allocation of indirect labor

Next we worked with the client and actually audited the press performance compared to the assumptions. We reached four conclusions:

1. The useful remaining life of the printing press was three years less than standard.
2. The press was being used for only one shift—the standard was for two shifts.
3. The printing press was printing 30 percent fewer sheets of paper per hour as compared to the standard assumption.
4. The accumulative downtime for the press was one hour more than standard.

After calculating the adjusted standards for the printing press, we revised the hourly operational cost of the printing press—it was $245 per hour! Remember, the business was selling this hour for $200. After discovering the true hourly rate, we then applied this process of review to all significant standard costs per machine, per product line, that were included in the past twelve months' adjusted net sales.

You can imagine what the owner and management team said: "We have adjusted sales, and now the costs to produce these sales are *greater*!"

At this stage, we will ask an owner to start examining the BMM process from his or her perspective. In this case, the owner said, "It costs me $45 more an hour than I am selling the hour of printing for. I am paying my salespeople 10 percent commission on the $200 revenue (sales) per hour!"

Case 5

Deception—Cost of Goods Sold

This client was an automotive after-market distributor of new parts and accessories for used cars. After auditing the company's standard costs compared to its monthly cost of goods sold, we found that the standard costs total was significantly more than the reported cost of goods sold. The owner had no explanation.

We then audited the current report for inventory that listed all standard products by their standard costs. This inventory report consisted of

- ➢ Raw materials
- ➢ Work in process
- ➢ Finished goods

Based on the company's methodology of standard costing, the following costs were allocated to the standard products based on percentage of completion:

- ➢ Freight costs
- ➢ Raw materials
- ➢ Direct labor
- ➢ Indirect labor
- ➢ Manufacturing overhead

This audit of the inventory report disclosed that millions of dollars had been accumulated in the balance sheet. We found that the company's CFO was deferring actual monthly cost of goods sold to the balance sheet for inventory work in process. We also found that the CFO underreported cost of goods sold because he feared that he would be terminated by the owner for not understanding why the business was losing money.

The owner knew his borrowing on his asset-based working capital loan was increasing, but he did not know why. Now that this information was disclosed, we compared the actual product standard cost to the company's pricing model and found the company was selling products at prices lower than the pricing guidelines specified. The owner had no knowledge that these procedures were being followed by his sales department.

It is important at this point in the BMM process to remind you why the owners in these cases that I have shared were able to make significant changes in their businesses. The owners accepted that they were following methods that created the *pattern*, and they agreed that this *pattern* strategy no longer worked. With this discovery, the owners became willing to change and embrace the BMM process.

We are building a sales model . . . then a cost of goods model. We have not yet started to build a better business. We are still building the foundation.

– EIGHT –

Revised Production Planning Process

Preparation of Production Process Analysis (Step 4)

Now that you have completed the previous twelve months' adjusted sales analysis and the adjusted cost of goods sold analysis, it is time to prepare a production schedule. This production schedule is designed to be consistent with the prior year adjusted sales and cost of goods manufactured. You will also include your current open customer purchase orders in this production schedule.

Now that we have your sales, we can prepare PERT charts by major categories of products/services. This linear timeline series of charts begins when your customer places a purchase order.

The next thing to do is review your available inventory:

- ➢ Raw materials
- ➢ Work in process

- Finished goods

Once you have compiled this information, you will match available inventory to your open purchase orders. After this matching process is completed, you will find unmatched open purchase orders that cannot be filled.

Next you will schedule required sales to be produced from your BMM process adjusted sales figures. Again, we then match this expected production to the sales model production requirements. After this matching process is completed, you will find production orders that cannot be filled.

Then you will review your open purchase orders to buy raw material and match these open purchase orders with both your *unfilled* customer purchase orders and your *unfilled* production orders. Now you can determine what additional raw materials you need to purchase to match customer production orders.

When this segment of the production schedule is completed, the owner usually finds there are customer purchase orders or production orders that cannot be filled because the necessary raw materials will not be available in time to meet production deadlines. You have now completed your production process analysis.

To give insight into the value of preparing a production schedule, I will now share the story of a rubber company that was a client. We will also return to this case later in the book.

Case 6

The Rubber Cord Company

This business owner manufactured and distributed his rubber cord products to mass merchandisers. The rubber came from Malaysia, and the thread was sourced in other Asian markets. The manufacturing plant was in the US. When the owner had completed his production schedule, he discovered the following critical information:

- The business had an inadequate supply of the specified quality of rubber from Malaysia.
- The business had an inadequate supply of thread to match quality specifications to manufacture rubber cords.

The owner then reviewed labor manpower and equipment required to produce the products matching the production schedule and uncovered the following problems:

- The machines to manufacture the required production did not have sufficient capacity to produce the products demanded on time.
- Workers were unable to operate the machines required to manufacture the products due to insufficient training.

In addition, the production schedule revealed

- ➢ The threading machines were configured to make a different quality of rubber cord than that required by the production schedule.
- ➢ There was a shortage of trained labor to operate the reconfigured threading machines.

At this point, the rubber company owner was able to determine that given a proper quality of rubber and proper specified thread, the production capacity, per reconfigured threading machine, would improve hourly production by 20 percent. The owner then reviewed effective past downtime for these threading machines and found that they were down an average of three hours per every ten-hour shift. These were the reasons for the excessive downtime:

- ➢ There was a shortage of raw materials.
- ➢ Poor quality rubber caused threading machines to be shut down for repair.
- ➢ Poor repair and maintenance programs for the threading machines required maintenance and repair to be performed on weekend plant downtimes.
- ➢ Supervision for the night shift was poor.

- ➢ In some cases, threading machines were shut down on the night shift during rest breaks and meals.
- ➢ Production of small custom orders required a threading machine to be shut down so it could be specially reconfigured and then restarted.

As the rubber company case shows, preparation of a production schedule will disclose great opportunities that you can implement in your action plan to return your business to earning sustained pretax profits. In chapter 14, Development of Your Action Plan, I will discuss how the rubber company owner solved production interruptions caused by these shortages of raw materials.

–NINE–

The Cornerstone

Preparation of Previous Twelve Months' Customer Marginal Profit Contribution Analysis (Step 5)

Now that you know how to prepare an adjusted sales projection for the following twelve months, in this chapter you will see how to determine marginal profit contributions for approximately 80 percent of your customers. From our work in previous chapters we have determined the following:

- Total sales by customer
- Total sales by customer product or service category
- Actual customer selling prices as compared to your pricing guidelines for products and services
- Total marketing and selling expenses per salesperson

At this juncture in the BMM process, there are many reasons to compute a customer's marginal profit contribution for the previous twelve months. The first is that once all the computations are completed for at least 80 percent of the customers, it is usually the first time that a business owner becomes aware of the percentage of profit contribution or dollar contribution by any customer for any one year.

In a previous chapter, I shared the case of the business owner who believed that a 50 percent markup meant a 50 percent gross profit. After we reviewed most of his customers' marginal profit contributions for the previous year, however, the owner was shocked to discover that many of his core customers had a minimum or negative marginal profit contribution. The owner was doubly dismayed because many of these core customers with poor performance were part of his sales strategy to increase sales volume by reducing product prices for the purpose of obtaining incremental profits.

Just think for a moment what has happened to this owner. First he determined a selling price for his product by cost-led pricing. In his case, he believed his product cost markup was higher than actually realized. Then he further reduced his prices believing that the increased volume of sales would create an incremental profit. So when this owner saw the results of his customer marginal profit contributions, the poor results were more than he could cope with.

As you have probably guessed, I am a great admirer of Peter Drucker. He once said that a time of turbulence is actually one of the greatest opportunities for those who can accept, understand, and exploit the new realities facing them. In his experience, though, the key to triumphing over such a challenge was the willingness to face reality.

This owner clearly had to face reality. He knew some of the causes of the turbulence in his business. As in our first case, part of their growth strategy was to obtain major new customers to become anchors for these new distribution centers, so they offered these potential anchor customers reduced prices to obtain incremental profits with increased sales volume. When we prepared the customer marginal profit contribution for these new anchor customers, however, the results disclosed that they all had negative marginal profit contributions and that the new distribution centers were operating at losses. That was the reality the two owners had to face.

I've also seen the need to face reality in my career in the corporate world. When I worked at the aeromotive company, the business had substantial quality problems. In one case, a jumbo jet engine was in the test cell after completion of its repairs, but it had not been properly secured in its required harnesses. During testing, it came free of the harnesses, and the customer's jet engine was destroyed with substantial damage to the test cell.

The customer was responsible for the final walk around to determine the security of the engine before connecting the final diagnosis instruments. In this case, however, the customer claimed the aeromotive business was responsible for the costs. You can imagine this customer's marginal profit (loss) contribution after allocating these associated losses to it. That was a huge reality check for all of us at the time.

I am sharing these thoughts with you at this time because as you go forward you will discover that you also have underperforming customers, and these underperforming customers will have poor marginal profit contributions. *It is important for you to expect turbulence as these owners did.* The reality may be difficult for you to confront, but turbulence in your business becomes a catalyst to proceed, to build to prosper. I am confident that success waits for you.

As we progress in the BMM process, the procedures require considerable diligence to obtain the detail necessary to complete our work. Initially owners do not believe that they have adequate records or all the time necessary to complete the various analyses required. However, I have not experienced a situation yet where an owner could not ultimately accomplish the tasks required.

—TEN—

Pricing Methodology Principle

Preparation of Pricing Analysis (Step 6)

Before we can create an action plan that will give you the hope you need to build your business to prosper, it is critical for you to become firmly rooted in pricing. In chapter 3, I reported what Drucker said about cost-led pricing and his belief that this methodology should be used by twenty-first century businesses. *This same pricing methodology is one of the primary principles taught by the BMM process that I have successfully applied for many years!*

Just as Henry Ford did, every business owner must first determine a reasonable price that the buyer will pay for a product. Ford is reputed to have said that he could sell the Model T at such a low price only because it earns such a nice profit. This price-led costing methodology is the exact opposite of cost-led pricing. With price-led costing, you determine the market price and then calculate all costs so that after adding those costs, the selling price will yield a 10 percent pretax profit. *In cost-led pricing, you determine your costs and then mark up your costs to result in an adequate return on investment.* Most business owners believe that a 10 percent return on their investment is sufficient.

These differences in costing methodologies are crucial for you to distinguish. In your marginalized business, it is necessary that you change your thinking and choose to build your business on price-led costing strategy. Otherwise it will be impossible for you to earn a 10 percent pretax profit return on your business's annualized sales!

Case 7

The Cookie Company

The cookie business had a profit improvement goal of $20,000,000, which had appeared unattainable. The cookie company had a previous twelve month statement of operating loss of $12,000,000, and the adjusted sales for the previous twelve months was $80,000,000 for the stores owned by the franchise company. Ten percent of the $80,000,000 in sales was $8,000,000. The previous year's operating loss of $12,000,000 plus this $8,000,000 pretax profit goal created a $20,000,000 profit improvement goal.

We analyzed the costs of the business including operating costs, personnel costs, product ingredient costs, and staff training and development costs and their efficiencies and analyzed the terms and conditions of the premise leases. We could not find any significant cost savings with the company's professional team. At that point, the entire management team thought that the company should be liquidated. The owners had lost all hope.

However we were not finished with the BMM process. We asked the owners and professional team if they thought the company had any other values. They said they did not! We then introduced our concept of intellectual properties and listed what we believed the company had created:

1. Customer loyalty—Most stores had many repeat customers who brought in-town guests
2. Highest quality product—Hot, excellent-tasting chocolate chip cookies
3. Good locations—Convenient store sites

We then returned to the intellectual property assessment. The owners said it reminded them of the story they tell potential franchisees in the franchisee prospectus, stating that the franchise owner could rely on the experience of a customer coming into the store and buying a hot chocolate chip cookie. The franchise company said this because it was true and to encourage potential franchisees that their future franchise had customers waiting to buy their chocolate chip cookies.

This was the opening we were hoping for. Whenever we analyze intellectual properties, this always happens. We then asked the owners if they saw value in this chocolate chip cookie experience, and they said that the experience is more important than the price to their customer, so we suggested they increase the size of their chocolate chip cookie by three ounces and increase the price to 97 cents from 47 cents for the new size of cookie. The owners agreed, with the franchisor and franchisees increasing prices to 97 cents per chocolate chip cookie. With this price increase, we exceeded the $20,000,000 profit improvement goal for the following twelve months.

Admittedly this is an exceptional case because the solution required a change only in cookie size and price. Nonetheless I believe the Cookie Case makes the point for you regarding the value of price-led costing. The BMM process led these owners from potential liquidation to sustainable pretax profits. Can you imagine if the owners had priced their cookie based upon their customers' experience (price-led costing) when they initially opened? Their pricing would have been consistent with their claims in the franchisee offering prospectus, but most important, they would have exceeded earning 10 percent of sales as a pretax profit goal annually from the start. Then the cookie company would have accumulated sufficient shareholder equity and the company franchisor could have had significant funds available for further innovation!

— ELEVEN —

Revised General and Administrative Expenses/Revised Statement of Operating Profit or Loss

Preparation of Previous Twelve Months' Adjusted General and Administrative Expense Analysis (Step 7)

Preparation of Previous Twelve Months' Adjusted Statement of Operating Profit or Loss (Step 8)

In this chapter, you will prepare adjustments to your previous twelve months' general and administrative expenses. Then you will prepare your previous twelve months' adjusted statement of operating profit or loss. Several adjustments are required to your general and administrative expenses because future expenses will increase, including items such as

- Premiums for your blanket general liability insurance
- Premiums for your workers' compensation insurance

- ➢ Rent
- ➢ Interest costs and penalty fees from a secured asset-based lender
- ➢ Health insurance premiums for employees
- ➢ Travel and entertainment costs for senior management
- ➢ Legal fees
- ➢ Accounting fees
- ➢ Human resource development costs

Once you have factored in all of these, you have completed your adjusted general and administrative expenses analysis for your future twelve-month period.

Now we will prepare your previous twelve months' adjusted statement of operating profit or loss. Be aware that this adjusted statement will result in a loss.

This is an important step because this pretax loss will be incorporated into your profit improvement goal. Before we start your action plan, we will review your core intellectual properties. These intellectual properties will give you the confidence and the foundation to create solutions in your action plan. In your action plan, you will discover commitments for change to be implemented to return your business to sustained profitability. To prepare you for your review of your intellectual properties and action plan, you need to take your previous twelve-month results of your statement of operating profit or loss. Through adjustments you will convert that statement to the adjusted statement of operating profit or loss.

Now you can start to prepare your adjusted statement of operating profit or loss. At this point, your business will be marginalized. The previous twelve months' adjusted statement of operating profit or loss will show a loss.

First refer to your previous adjusted twelve-month schedules that you have already completed:

- ➢ Adjusted sales analysis
- ➢ Adjusted marketing and selling expense analysis
- ➢ Adjusted cost of goods sold analysis
- ➢ Production process analysis
- ➢ Customer marginal profit contribution analysis
- ➢ Pricing analysis
- ➢ Adjusted general and administrative expense analysis

You will use these analyses to make adjustments to your previous twelve months' actual performance of operating profit or loss as follows:

1. You will replace the last twelve months' actual sales with your BMM adjusted sales.
2. You will replace the last twelve months' actual marketing and selling expenses with the projected marketing and selling expense analysis.
3. You will adjust the last twelve months' cost of goods sold with any adjustments that you found.

4. You will make adjustments and reduce your customers' sale prices that you found when you prepared your customers' marginal profit contributions.
5. You will make cost adjustments for increased material costs discovered when you prepared your production analysis.
6. You will reduce prices from customers who received previous price concessions.
7. You will make adjustments to increase future general and administrative expenses.

You have now completed an adjusted statement of operating profit or loss after applying all these adjustments to your previous twelve months statement of operating profit or loss.

This following case about a client who owned a pizza company will help you at this stage of preparation as you get ready to work on your profit improvement goal.

Case 8

The Pizza Company Owner

This client was a regional pizza manufacturer that sold pizzas to institutional accounts through food brokers. The business was well over thirty years old, and the owner wanted to expand. However, his business had become marginalized, so he was very willing to accept my help.

The BMM process revealed that the previous twelve months' adjusted statement of operating profit or loss consisted of a statement of operating loss for the preceding twelve months of approximately $6,500,000 as well as added adjustments found during the BMM process of $2,500,000, for a total of $9,000,000.

The owner's profit improvement goal then consisted of earning 10 percent pretax profits on adjusted annual sales from the previous twelve months, plus the recovery of his previous twelve months' operating loss.

The owner's previous twelve months' adjusted sales were $55,000,000; 10 percent of these sales then became an expected pretax profit return of $5,500,000. Therefore his profit improvement goal became the $5,500,000 plus recovering his pretax loss of $9,000,000, for a total profit improvement goal of $14,500,000.

That is a staggering goal for any business owner to achieve! Therefore he had to develop an action plan sufficient to create $14,500,000 in commitments for change in profit improvements so his business could earn sustained pretax profits over the next twelve months of $5,500,000.

Before we started to help the owner create his action plan, we thoroughly reviewed the intellectual properties he had created in the business that would provide the foundation for finding solutions to return to earning sustained pretax profits. The intellectual properties we agreed on were

- Brand name—Amazing brand recognition by regional institutions
- Great quality and taste—Owner had his own recipe for pizzas
- Great delivery—Always on time, which was important since many institutional customers were schools
- Very dependable and skilled workforce
- Great vendors that provided the cheeses
- Great vendors that provided the dough ingredients

Based on the confidence we had in these intellectual properties, the owner decided to make a number of significant commitments for change in his action plan. He entered into new contracts with new food brokers to distribute his pizzas to additional new institutional customers. However, the business owner believed that he could preserve his current pricing and customers with his existing food brokers. The owner had additional production capacity and believed that with these new brokers and institutional customers he could earn marginal profits.

After he signed these new agreements, however, his current food brokers discovered what he had done and demanded the same lower prices as the new food brokers. Consequently we met with both the old and new food brokers. We asked each of them how they saw the future growth of the institutional pizza regional market. Most of them believed that the institutional market was asking for more variety than just cheese pizzas.

We then asked the food brokers if we reduced the pizza size by two inches (combined length and width) if the institutional customers would still buy the product. They were certain that this minor difference would not affect sales to their customers.

After several meetings with each food broker, the owner decided to determine if his plant could respond and meet the new demand in making the pizzas with increased production. He then studied the adjustments that would have to be made to change the size and possibly add other toppings. Shortly thereafter, the owner had developed a plan to reconfigure his plant production layout to manufacture the following:

- Cheese pizzas
- Sausage pizzas
- Pepperoni pizzas

We then went back and met separately with each food broker and, with the new mix of pizza styles and increased production capability, were able to negotiate revised contracts with increased prices for all of his food brokers. Given the increase in pizza prices and plant production and the savings of materials due to reduced pizza size, the food brokers were still able to sell additional pizzas to their institutional customers because of the variety now offered.

After his action plan was implemented, the business owner exceeded $6,000,000 in sustainable pretax profits for the next twelve months.

I trust this case gives you hope. As you continue working through the BMM process, do not become overwhelmed by the profit improvement goal you will create in the next chapter. You can rely upon your action plan to return your business to sustained profitability.

— TWELVE —

Profit Improvement Goal

Preparation of Profit Improvement Goal (Step 9)

In chapter 11, you applied the BMM process to prepare a previous twelve months' adjusted statement of operating profit or loss. If your business is marginalized, this statement will likely reflect a significant loss. Despite this loss, you need to move ahead to prepare your profit improvement goal. This computation consists of adding your prior year's adjusted operating loss and 10 percent of the sales from your previous twelve months' adjusted statement of operating profit or loss. The combined total becomes your profit improvement goal.

At this point, you have probably lost faith that you can restore your business to profitability. Your ability to make changes to reach your profit improvement goal seems overwhelming because you do not yet see the entire picture of your business.

In chapter 13, as you prepare an inventory of your intellectual properties, your hope will be restored, and you will have faith that your intellectual properties are the solution on which you can base decisions to restore your business to earning sustained profits.

To inspire you, I will now summarize a case that is an extraordinary example of an owner who set a staggering profit improvement goal, particularly in light of his business situation and the market conditions he faced. You will see how the BMM process helped reveal the intellectual properties that ultimately saved this business and led the owner to earn sustained pretax profits.

Case 9

The Residential Home Developer

We were engaged by the owner of this business because his partner had just committed suicide out of despair that their business appeared that it could not be saved. The business consisted of three facets:

- ➢ One large development of homes in different stages of completion
- ➢ One large development of homes where all the offsite work was completed and pads were prepared for framing to start

- ➢ One large development of homes at the planning/city approval stage

After we applied the BMM process, the profit improvement goal for the business exceeded $15,000,000, consisting of both the developer's previous twelve-month adjusted statement of operating loss of $7,500,000 and 10 percent of $75,000,000 in sales. The developer's previous twelve months' adjusted statement of operating profit or loss recorded a loss that exceeded $7,500,000.

During our work, we also discovered the following issues facing his business:

- ➢ Prior union subcontractors for his homes under construction were purposely sabotaging the efforts of new nonunion workers, for example, reversing the plumbing to turn hot water to cold.
- ➢ Homeowners in this development had lengthy lists of items to be fixed.
- ➢ Underground sewer lines had not been properly engineered for appropriate connections.
- ➢ Storm drains were clogged with cement placed there by the union workers.
- ➢ Interest rates and fees from the secured lender financing the development nearly completed

and the one about to start construction were reaching an all-time industry high.

- Interest rates and points for new buyer conventional mortgage loans were reaching an all-time industry high.
- The secured lender was accelerating payment of secured loans on all three of the developer's projects due to violation of several loan agreement covenants.
- Potential homebuyers could not sell their existing homes.

The secured lender was calling the loan not only because the developer was in violation of loan agreement covenants but also because at this time in the marketplace many developers were walking away from their home development projects. The secured lender wanted to mitigate its exposure to this developer because of the potential risk that the owner might also walk away from his obligations.

Can you imagine the patience that this developer had to go through the BMM process only to find out that his profit improvement goal was $15,000,000 and, worse yet, he was facing tenuous conditions in the financial market and the single-family home industry?

I assured this developer early on and often, just as I have you, that his solution rested in his intellectual properties. As we began the process of inventorying intellectual properties, I asked the owner what he believed had value in his single-family home development business. Here is only a partial list of what he cited:

1. The architectural engineering drawings of our homes have brand recognition.
2. The architectural engineering drawings of our single-family homes have been approved by the city planning review board.
3. Our available inventory of single-family homes is in high demand by buyers.
4. Our architectural engineering specifications offer homeowners efficient and cost-effective use of gas and electricity.
5. The planning and review board of the city is near approval of our newest development of single-family homes.
6. Our management team and new, nonunion contractors are the best in the region.
7. I had a long-standing relationship with his interim-construction secured lender.

8. I had a long-standing relationship with the single-family home mortgage lender.
9. I have an excellent marketing and selling organization that has sold our homes in the region for several years.
10. Other than homeowner concerns in the development near completion, past homeowners in the region would testify to the quality and unusual designs of our homes.
11. In my new development where the offsite work and prepared pads are completed, I do not have to build model homes because prospective buyers could view existing models in my completed development.
12. I have the trust of the city planning board, city inspectors, regional realty board, and owners of my existing homes in the region.

I could continue with his intellectual properties, but these twelve intellectual properties now became the very foundation for this developer to find solutions to return his business to earning sustained pretax profits.

I will now summarize some of the results of the developer's action plan and his continuing commitments for change:

- ➢ The developer met with his interim construction loan secured lender and submitted a plan to increase the sale prices of his homes and reduce the construction costs.
- ➢ The developer met with his interim construction loan secured lender and submitted a production schedule of completion for construction of each lot and home.
- ➢ The developer met with his interim construction lender and submitted a selling schedule of expected completion date for each escrow to close by lot number.
- ➢ The developer met with the single-family home mortgage lender and paid a fee to obtain a commitment for future homebuyers to secure the lender's financing.
- ➢ The developer arranged single-family home financing for him to buy the homes that future homebuyers would purchase and then rent these houses he bought until the single-family home market started to improve.

The developer then presented his action plan to his marketing and real estate selling agents. Within a year and a half, the first two projects had closed, and his new project was nearing approval by the city planning board. *This single-family home developer significantly exceeded his profit improvement goal of $15,000,000.* The new homebuyers had no concerns with the increased prices for the homes they bought, and they offered to sell their homes at reasonable prices to the developer. I should note that the profits earned from the sale of his rental properties are not included in the above figure.

In chapter 14, I will discuss with you the process of creating your action plan. You will develop adequate commitments for changes to be implemented in your business that are sufficient to reach your profit improvement goal. These changes are determined by your intellectual properties.

—THIRTEEN—

Intellectual Properties: Your Foundation for Growth

Preparation of Inventory of Your Intellectual Properties (Step 10)

Welcome to hope! It has taken time for you to reach this chapter. When you determined your profit improvement goal, you probably went into a state of despair. However, earlier in the book, we discussed how the owners in the Cookie Case had given up hope after reviewing their operating costs, and it was only when we helped them discover their intellectual properties that they saw a path to prosperity. They remembered the initial value that they believed their franchise brought to their customers. The experience of eating a delicious, warm chocolate chip cookie had created loyal, repeat customers who brought friends and relatives to the stores to enjoy the same experience.

In chapter 4, Accelerated Decline of Life Cycles, you first realized that your business life cycle had declined and had become marginalized. Now even though you have a profit improvement goal, you are not able see how to make all the necessary changes to your business to accomplish this goal. You are thinking that if you knew how to make those changes you would not need to read this book. I have continually assured you that your solution rests within your intellectual properties. Your intellectual properties will extend your businesses life cycle! Your intellectual properties are the foundation for you to restore life to your marginalized business!

Here is an inventory of the five core intellectual properties that will return your business to earning sustained pretax profits:

- Trusting customers
- Loyal customers
- Excellent customer service
- Excellent quality products/services and timely delivery
- Channels of distribution

These five intellectual properties become the foundation of your action plan. Once you see the value in them, you will proceed to make changes to your business so you can build to prosper. To help you, let's return now to the rubber cord company, whose owner discovered the inherent value of the intellectual properties he had created in his business.

This business owner manufactured and distributed his rubber cord products to mass merchandisers. The rubber came from Malaysia, and the thread was sourced in other Asian markets. The manufacturing plant was in the US. The business owner was in default of his loan agreement covenants, and his asset-based lender initially wanted the business owner to find a new lender and pay off its loan. The owner's lender referred him to us.

After we applied the BMM process, the profit improvement goal was $8,000,000. The previous twelve months' adjusted sales were approximately $50,000,000. The profit improvement goal consisted of a previous year adjusted pretax loss of $3,000,000 and a 10 percent goal of adjusted sales of $50,000,000 as a pretax profit goal of $5,000,000.

The owner was unsettled by his profit improvement goal, but we were able to keep him focused on the end result. As he continued with the BMM process, we reviewed with him his key intellectual properties. First his mass merchandiser customers were strategically placed throughout the US to sell to their retail customers who preferred his company's brand of rubber cord.

Second the owner had created an extraordinary channel of distribution to get products to market. The business owner had relied on cost-led pricing, however, and had begun to reduce the prices of his products in hopes of earning incremental profits by increasing sales volume.

During the BMM process of preparation of the previous twelve months' adjusted sales analysis, cost of goods manufactured analysis, and production process analysis, we had discovered the following:

- ➢ The business had an inadequate supply of the specified quality of rubber from Malaysia.
- ➢ The business had an inadequate supply of thread to match quality specifications to manufacture rubber cords.

The owner then reviewed labor, manpower, and equipment required to produce the products matching the production schedule and uncovered the following problems:

- ➢ The business had an inadequate supply of the proper grade of rubber from Malaysia.
- ➢ The business had an inadequate supply of thread.
- ➢ The threading machines were partially configured to make a different quality of rubber hose product than projected.
- ➢ Due to high customer demand, lower-quality rubber was being purchased from vendors to gain faster delivery times from Asia.

Suffice to say, an $8,000,000 profit improvement goal is a healthy target to accomplish.

When we prepared the product marginal profit contributions, we found that one size of rubber cord exceeded the required marginal profit contribution threshold. This particular size made up about 40 percent of sales volume. For this size, the company had adequate raw material to fill open orders already en route to the plant.

Because the mass merchandisers were loyal customers, we were able to get them to agree to sell only this one size for approximately six months. During this period, the company was able to sustain 80 percent of the projected sales and maintain the favorable pricing. Meanwhile the business owner went to Malaysia and found new rubber cord vendors with great quality and lower costs. The owner then negotiated new thread contracts with new Asian vendors at reduced costs. In addition, the threading machines were set up to efficiently produce top-quality products with very little scrap.

The channel of distribution of using mass merchandisers to sell the rubber cords to satisfied customers was the key intellectual property that saved this business from liquidation.

After six months, other rubber cord sizes were brought back to the market at higher prices. These higher prices were determined by *price-led costing*. The mass merchandisers and the customers were grateful to now have additional size choices after the six-month delay. Needless to say, even the business owner was shocked when his company exceeded the profit improvement goal of $8,000,000. And again, this was accomplished because the owner had built exceptional intellectual properties that he relied on to return his business to earning sustained pretax profits.

As the rubber company case shows, preparation of an inventory of your intellectual properties will disclose great opportunities that you can implement in your action plan to return your company to sustained pretax profits. It's your turn to build to prosper now!

—FOURTEEN—

Developing Your Action Plan

The purpose of the action plan is to create and implement commitments for change to your business that will meet or exceed your profit improvement goal and return your business to earning sustained pretax profits.

We have discussed how overwhelmed you may feel after your profit improvement goal is computed. However, after preparing the summary of your core intellectual properties, you will have hope because you can see their inherent value. You are encouraged that solutions may exist that will help your business reach its profit improvement goal.

The BMM process relies on these intellectual properties to help find solutions that become commitments for change that, when implemented in your business, will help accomplish the profit improvement goal.

The action plan is a numbered list with item after item of solutions, called commitments for change, to be implemented. Usually the owner and the management team participate in creating these solutions, and either the owner or a designated management team member is chosen to oversee this action plan and report weekly on progress being made toward the implementation of the commitments for change. Often some of the changes do not work or the changes provide improvements that are less than expected. If this occurs, the owner and management team will reconvene and determine new solutions until their profit improvement goal is accomplished.

The best way for you to become more acquainted with the specifics of an action plan is to observe the BMM process in practice in the following case.

Case 10

The Appliance Company

In chapter 3, I summarized the business of this regional retail appliance company. As you will recall, this owner believed that he had a good pricing strategy determined by a break-even analysis that was structured to provide adequate pretax profits for his company in its competitive market place. Most importantly, the owner was determined that his business could cross the threshold to profitability by greater sales volume at reduced prices. He believed that he could pull in more customers through a major advertising and promotion campaign on regional radio stations and TV networks. The combined cost of these programs was approximately $10,000,000 a year.

This appliance company had six outlets, including the corporate headquarters located in its marquee retail store. We replaced our traditional BMM process preparation of customer marginal profit contribution analysis with a six-store marginal profit contribution analysis. The owner and his management team struggled with allocating the $10,000,000 promotional costs to each store. After revisiting this critical assessment several times, the owner was 90 percent confident with the final allocation of program costs, only to discover that after this allocation each store became unprofitable for its previous twelve-month period. The owner could not believe this at first but did finally accept these results. At this point in the BMM process, the owner was quite disappointed with the results of these detailed analyses of his stores.

Before we started the action plan, we reviewed with the owner what we all had agreed were the key intellectual properties in his business:

1. Customers trusted the owner.

2. Customers were loyal and would return to buy more products or services.
3. Customers counted on store service for installation and repairs in their homes.
4. Customers loved visiting stores and spending time with the well-trained employees.
5. Customers had come to expect product and were confident that their choice of a product would be in the inventory and available that day for delivery.

These intellectual properties had been created by the owner over the past thirty years. I asked the owner if it made any sense to him that his customers all were more than satisfied and yet he was not making any pretax profits. He responded, "I believe my customers will be willing to pay higher prices for the goods and services that we sell them because my business provides them so much added value."

Now that we had this owner's understanding, we could go about developing our action plan. In this case, though, we created seven separate action plans, one for each store and one for the corporate headquarters.

We held separate meetings for each store with its management and evaluated product turnover. In many cases, the product turnover did not meet minimum expectations. When we separated product categories and determined the marginal profit contribution per major category, we discovered that various stores, for the same category of product, were making different marginal profit contributions. We found negative marginal profit contributions. We learned that the sales per employee varied widely per store as did the average customer purchase per store. We found that employee overtime was significantly different per store.

Now, with all this information at hand, we worked with the owner and his CFO to construct a store model that would yield a 10 percent pretax profit on an annual basis. We made seasonal adjustments for slow months and for peak sale periods in the summer and Christmas season. In this modeling process, we did the following:

- Increased prices per various product or service categories by an average of 9 percent
- Eliminated 90 percent of overtime
- Closed two stores that were near enough to the marquee store on the belief that at least 80 percent of those store customers would drive to the marquee store

- ➢ Balanced the proper number of employees for expected store traffic
- ➢ Increased service fees by 20 percent
- ➢ Eliminated $6,000,000 of the $10,000,000 of promotional costs

This modeling process was the beginning of the action plan. We then held sessions with each store management team to submit our model and then created their action plan with them. As the management team agreed to an action, that action was written into their plan. This action item became a commitment for change that required implementation.

Each action item had a dollar value determined to be saved or earned over the following twelve months. Saved meant a cost that was included in the previous twelve months' adjusted statement of operating profit or loss per store or headquarters. Earned meant increased sales (price increases) with no cost increase. As an example, an action item in one store was to increase prices in one product category by 9 percent.

At this time, we had all the tools necessary to start our action plan. The business profit improvement goal exceeded $16,000,000. Each store had more than one hundred action items in its action plan. Designated executives were assigned responsibility for ensuring these action items were implemented. The total number of action items for all the regional stores and headquarters exceeded one thousand. Most of the time a business does not require more than one hundred action items, but this case helps make the point regarding the precision required to develop and implement a successful action plan.

Please remember that our starting point in developing an action plan is the previous twelve months' adjusted statement of operating profit or loss. In this case, the previous twelve months' adjusted statement of operating profit or loss was a loss of $4,000,000. The adjusted future twelve months' sales were $120,000,000. Attaining a 10 percent return on sales of $120,000,000 results in a pretax profit of $12,000,000. Thus the profit improvement goal for this owner was $16,000,000.

As I always tell clients, you can trust the BMM process! This owner exceeded his profit improvement goal of $16,000,000 in the following twelve months. This meant that the business recovered in profits the $4,000,000 loss and also earned pretax profits of $12,000,000.

I should note here that the last items in any action plan become the CFO's responsibility. After applying the action items to the previous twelve months' adjusted statement of operating profit or loss, the CFO constructs a new statement of operating profit or loss. This statement becomes the new forecast by month. These monthly projections are then used to create monthly cash flows and monthly balance sheets. These projected financial statements become the financial support structure of your "build to prosper business plan." This business plan relies on your action plan for at least the first six months of your business going forward.

As we move to the Innovation section of the book, I want to encourage you that this successful case I have just shared can happen for you! As you learn more about the core of your intellectual properties, you will be able to construct action plans to build on these intellectual properties and reap the harvest of your inheritance.

INNOVATION

— FIFTEEN —

Inheritance

Why have we been struggling to prosper? Is our economic model of capitalism contrary to God's economic model in the heavens? Have we been taught economic theories that were purposely designed to lead us into marginalizing our businesses throughout America? Are the Chinese responsible? Has China implemented a strategic plan over the past twenty years to become the banker of the United States? Today we owe China more than one trillion dollars, and yet there is no existing solution to pay back the principal. So what possibly went wrong? Can we blame economic theory?

Let's go back in American history. In 1913, a century ago, Henry Ford earned pretax profits of approximately $26,000,000 (these are dollars in 1913 values). Ford certainly had his financial problems too. Ford's automotive plants were in the process of installing assembly lines, but Ford found that it was taking his management time to invest in hiring new employees and training existing workers. Employees did not like working on the assembly line because they found it boring. Ford and his management team discovered that they were interviewing one thousand applicants just to hire one hundred workers.

To solve this problem, Ford chose to substantially increase hourly pay once an employee reached certain required levels of training, with hourly measurements of performance that included the ability to speak English. After implementing these new procedures, the Ford management team only had to interview one hundred applicants to hire one hundred employees. People wanted to work for Ford, and they stood in lines to be considered for the opportunity.

In 1914, Ford paid out additional wages to his workforce, including incentives of approximately $12,000,000. When asked why he did this, he replied that by increasing the pay of his workforce, each employee could then buy a Model T Ford!

So what happened to Ford's workforce as many workers were eventually replaced by the assembly line? These hard-working immigrants became mechanics to repair the Model T or carpenters and other types of craftsmen to help construct new homes, buildings, schools, streets, and gas stations. Employment in this country became an exciting expectation by Americans. Unprecedented economic growth continued into the late 1920s. American business was at its best!

Additionally Henry Ford helped create the automobile industry that provided reasonably priced cars throughout America. He determined the price of a Model T Ford by price-led costing methods, and *his pretax profit returns were sufficient to meet investment requirements for future innovations.*

Ford built upon his innovations. He constructed more plants with assembly lines. He developed a more highly trained and efficient workforce. He increased channels of distribution, including more car dealers to sell his Model T. He paid fair wages so communities could be built to support his workforce. These innovations continued to create more jobs within the Ford empire and in the broader American economy.

The Wal-Mart Model Introduces Marginalization

Ford's innovation strategies became models of running a business profitably in stark contrast to those in America starting in the late 1970s. Let us examine what happened in that time period. First Sam Walton, founder of Wal-Mart, introduced mass merchandising to America. He opened up stores that focused on selling volumes of low-cost products to his customers. His mission back then was to sell only

American-made products. His stores were initially located in the Southeast, where the textile and apparel industries had invested in innovations over the previous century to create equipment that would enable companies to respond to customer demand and quality expectations. Amazingly, however, the Chinese began to enter the marketplace. After attending our universities and schools and working at our textile mills learning how to manufacture apparel, they returned to China to build a manufacturing industry using the technology they learned from us.

The Chinese then developed a market strategy to sell mass volumes of garments at highly reduced prices to Wal-Mart. They could sell at significantly reduced prices because they could deploy a workforce at low hourly rates. These hourly rates were similar to rates initially paid by Ford more than sixty years earlier before he raised the wages of his employees.

In describing what happened with the Chinese and garment manufacturing, I have dissected a subsection of the overall collapse of various industries in America that have now been replaced by those in China and India to serve as an example from which we must learn.

During the early 1980s, many business owners in this country chose to rely on the eight trusted economic theories to assist them in response to these changing conditions in the American marketplace. You may have owned your own business at that time and sold your products directly to Wal-Mart or to customers that sold to Wal-Mart. You probably found that you were increasingly in competition with China and India because Wal-Mart had made the decision to buy the lowest-priced product offered to them. This meant that they no longer sold only American-made products but those manufactured in Asia as well.

Today it is reasonable to assume that 80 percent of Wal-Mart's products are imported from Asia. Therefore, when you or your customer tried to determine how to keep your annual sales to Wal-Mart intact, you and your management went back to your break-even analysis training. You believed in the incremental profit contribution economic theory, so you reduced your prices.

Remember, you already had expectations of a pretax profit based on the economic theory of a reasonable return on investment. Consequently you have accelerated the decline of your product life cycles and started your business on the course of being marginalized. If you are like many business owners dealing with this problem, you are continuing to try to minimize the effect of these price reductions by reducing your workforce and expecting more from existing employees. You may even freeze hiring, cease promotions and salary increases, cut training, and make very limited investment in innovations.

These limited investments are applied to operating efficiencies with the purpose of reducing your costs, and with these efficiencies, you then terminate more of your workforce. Ironically the workforce gradually being terminated continues to buy products at discounted prices from Wal-Mart. They actually become the very consumers who put themselves out of work by preferring to buy lesser-quality, price-discounted products from Wal-Mart and other mass merchandising chains that operate on this principle. As the unemployment of our precious workforce increases, Wal-Mart and some of its counterparts continue to establish record sales.

So let's review where we are at present: Mass merchandise chains are successful. The people of China and India desire to be prosperous. Business owners in China and India are making marginal profits. In America, we have lost 6.3 million manufacturing jobs between January 1990 and January 2010, the industry's low point, a 36 percent decline according to the Bureau of Labor Statistics. The Chinese have a trillion dollars in US government securities with no evident method of repayment of these securities. We have a record dollar amount of capital not being released to invest in American businesses for future innovations.

Now imagine if the following path had been taken in the early 1980s: Retailers, mass merchandisers, and others chose to sell only American-made products. The Chinese took our technology home and, just as Henry Ford did, increased product prices sufficient to earn 10 percent pretax profits on sales and increased workforce wages. The Chinese workforce bought the products they made. The same method of industrialization and economic growth that occurred in America would have occurred in China. If the Chinese business owners would have substantially increased the wages of their workforce, the workers would then become consumers. Just as Ford's workforce became consumers, new retail stores in China would be opened to sell merchandise manufactured in China. New buildings, new jobs, new homes, and new communities would have been developed on the Chinese mainland.

Today the US has 313 million people. China's population is approaching 1.5 billion, almost five times that of this country. China's economy would be the largest in the world today if its workforce became consumers. The Chinese would not have invested one trillion dollars in our debt—and we would not owe them a trillion dollars! The American business owner's pretax profits would have been reinvested in innovations that grow our economy. The American workforce would have manufactured the goods, and our citizens here would have bought them. In addition, China might have joined in supporting humanitarian programs throughout the world to care for oppressed people.

Innovation: Create a New Economic Model

Business owners can rethink their growth strategy. Possibly we can be innovative and build a new enhanced economic model where wealth becomes the by-product, not the goal. An example of this is Muhammad Yunus. In 1983, Muhammad Yunus established Grameen, a bank devoted to helping the poorest of Bangladesh with microloans. Twenty-three years later, he won the Nobel Peace Prize for work in eradicating poverty. Business owners can implement a new economic theory of earning a reasonable return on their investment and applying a return of 10 percent of pretax profits of sales. Then sufficient profits will become available to them to reinvest in innovation, and prosperity will return to America as business owners rebuild their companies for growth that will last into future generations.

I believe the current breakdown in our economy is due to the fact that we no longer stand strong in our trust in God. Our currency says, “In God we trust,” but that trust seems not to be in our hearts. Judging by what is happening to our economy, could the prosperity curve be directly related to our trust in God?

We can learn a lot from American farmers. They believe every day that they will reap what they sow. American farmers depend on their faith. They believe that the seeds they plant will grow into a flourishing harvest.

In the past you too had faith. You brought new products to market, built a workforce, promoted people, trained people, provided them employee benefits and pension plans, contributed money to their communities to support their families and children, and probably supported a variety of charities through contributions from your company. But today your business is marginalized.

To return to prosperity, you need to trust once again—not trust in foreign countries or even trust in yourself—but trust in each other as we rebuild America on our founding values and reinvest in innovation that creates social values for your customers similar to Muhammad Yunus. My hope is that we can follow the example of the American farmer and apply the economic theory of sowing and reaping. And yes, it does require faith.

I am confident that your faith can be restored as you apply the BMM process to your business. The process will reveal to you the valuable resources in your existing business that you and others have planted. As you have seen, the BMM process helps you reap these previously planted seeds. I have chosen to call these seeds waiting to be harvested your *intellectual properties*.

These intellectual properties existing in your business can include any or all of the following:

- The trust that exists between you and your customer
- Your customers
- Your customers' marginal profit contribution
- The life expectancy of your products and services
- The quality of your products and services
- The culture of your business
- Your management team
- Your private data and demographic analysis of the markets that you support
- Your private assessment of your competitors
- Your brands
- Your strategies, methods, and processes to promote and advertise your products to prospective customers
- Your strategies, methods, and processes to sell your products to prospective customers
- Your marketing and salespeople.
- Your workforce
- The systems and procedures that you have created for your manufacturing process
- Your engineering staff and their designs, templates, and drawings created for the formulation of building products

- Your technology development process
- Your management information systems and supporting customer resource files
- Your channels of distribution—how you get your product to market
- Your relationships with your vendors

These intellectual properties have become your inheritance. They have tremendous value that can provide your business with hope for the future. Yes, at this moment you need faith that you can convert these intellectual properties, which are the legacy of your business, into prosperity. By prosperity, I mean sustainable pretax profits sufficient to be reinvested in your business. In the next chapter, Inheritance Converted to Prosperity, I share three cases of businesses that I hope encourage you with their evidence of success in discovering intellectual properties.

—SIXTEEN—

Inheritance Converted to Prosperity

In the previous chapter, I showed how the intellectual properties of your business have become your inheritance. As you apply the BMM process, these intellectual properties will be revealed, and you will find insight into these values. Your understanding of these intellectual properties will help you convert them into sustainable pretax profits sufficient to reinvest in your business for growth.

To demonstrate this truth, I now share three cases of clients. In the first case, you will see how the BMM process disclosed that some significant customers had low marginal profit contributions. These customers were large national accounts that had recently become customers. Your thought will be that the owner of the business had relied on the economic theory of reducing prices to increase volume. However, as noted before, buying customers doesn't work. And yes, the owner did reduce prices to increase sales volume.

However, you will see that by applying the BMM process, we were able to improve the customers' marginal profit contributions, enabling the business to earn 10 percent of sales as pretax profits. We effectively changed the costing method from cost-led costing to price-led costing by establishing new pricing guidelines. This change was important because we converted these underperforming customers to very profitable accounts. With a sales strategy based on new pricing guidelines, the owners were so filled with hope that their enthusiasm was difficult to contain! They knew that their sales team could now go out and be competitive in the marketplace and bring in additional new major customers. These owners saw the value of the intellectual property of customer trust and how to convert it into sustainable pretax profits. This is an example of building on intellectual properties.

Case 11

The Owners Who Decided to Do Things Differently

This client manufactured and sold metal and wood screen doors throughout the US, direct to the retailer. Its secured asset-based lender was concerned because the business was losing money and had not met certain loan agreement covenants. The lender asked the company to get help, and the owners retained us to help them return their business to profitability.

The business was seasonal. The owners believed that they had adequate purchase orders from their customers for the next busy season and believed that their business would return to profitability at that time. However, they told me that the lender did not share their optimism.

As we began our engagement, we found that 70 percent of sales were shipped between April and July. The company had two manufacturing plants, one for metal screen doors and the other for wood screen doors. We decided to prepare a BMM process for each of them because the manufacturing processes were different. Together the BMM processes had a combined profit improvement goal of $7,000,000.

We prepared the previous year adjusted sales analysis for each facility and then prepared manufacturing scheduled projections for the future twelve months. After reviewing these production schedules, the owners and their senior management asked, "What can we do differently?" Their willingness to look at their business through a new lens ignited thinking that ultimately led to an amazing turnaround in their bottom line. They began by looking at these facts:

- ➢ Direct labor costs and benefits were more than 40 percent of the total of cost of goods manufactured for the metal and wood screen doors.
- ➢ Manufacturing overhead/maintenance costs exceeded 15 percent of the total of cost of goods sold for the metal doors.
- ➢ Manufacturing scrap for the metal doors exceeded 20 percent of material costs.
- ➢ Manufacturing scrap for the wood doors exceeded 30 percent of material costs.
- ➢ Workers compensation claims and costs were double the standard for the industry.

The owners also looked at operational factors. Other than Christmas, the manufacturing plants worked one shift except for two ten-hour shifts a day during the months of April through July to respond to peak demand. However, the new production schedule based on adjusted net sales we had prepared according to the BMM process revealed that there would be a 30 percent decline in demand for both the metal and wood doors because two major customers from the previous year were no longer going to buy from the business.

In light of this reduced demand and wondering, "What could we do differently?" the owners and management team decided to implement the action plan we developed that required a major change in the production process. For the past twenty-five years the company's hourly employees and family members who were employees had used the same production process, equipment, and raw materials for both the metal and wood screen doors. Instead the owners now agreed to adopt a new manufacturing schedule that produced all the doors over a five-month period and also employ a significantly reduced workforce on a four-day, ten-hour per day workweek to support their nonseasonal production. One of the primary benefits of the four-day, ten-hour per day workweek was that the business could retain its experienced labor force.

Another answer to "What could we do differently?" resulted in a decision by the owners to store inventory in a warehouse and ship on demand to their mass merchandising customers. The business negotiated new agreements with some of its large customers who resold screens, granting them the ability to inventory the excess screens that the business produced. In turn, these customers received dating terms, which gave the business the ability to pay its receivables from these customers over extended payment terms.

Once the owners and their managers implemented these commitments for change, they saw immediate benefits that translated into pretax profits:

- ➢ Just-in-time delivery resulted in increased sales exceeding the adjusted net sales.
- ➢ Direct labor costs fell due to 40 percent lower benefit outlays.
- ➢ Machine maintenance costs dropped by 5 percent.
- ➢ Metal screen door scrap was reduced by 7 percent.
- ➢ Workers compensation insurance costs declined to the industry average.

After examining the scrap rate for the wood doors, we had also discovered that due to seasonality, the purchasing department often bought inferior lumber grades to meet production schedules. With the new production schedule, the business was now able to select a higher grade of lumber and maintain this standard, reducing lumber scrap from 30 percent to 10 percent.

Because of their willingness to implement all the commitments for change in our action plan, the owners were able to reduce their manufacturing costs on an annual basis by $5,000,000! Our entire profit improvement goal was set at $7,000,000, but we had already accomplished a savings of $5,000,000 just by making substantive changes to the manufacturing process.

Once we reconciled the production schedules to the products to be manufactured, we then determined new bill of material standard costs for all products. The reduction in manufacturing costs by an annualized $5,000,000 was reflected in significant reductions in the revised bill of material costs, which allowed the owners to review their pricing guidelines. Because reduced costs almost met the threshold improvements required for expected customers' marginal profit contribution goals, in many cases the business needed only to increase prices 3 to 7 percent for customers who had previously underperformed.

Before we started this engagement, the owner believed that he would have trouble just paying off his unsecured creditors if he were to liquidate his business. Remember, the profit improvement goal was $7,000,000. Now the business was earning $5,000,000 in pretax profits even before adding new customers and implementing innovations.

This company's profit improvement computation included a $2,000,000 pretax loss for the previous year just ended. Their adjusted previous twelve-month sales were $50,000,000. So now the business was establishing a new run rate of adding new sales and products as they were created. Can you imagine the projected pretax profit for the third year?

The Value of Customer Trust

The next case is another real-world situation that brings to light how a business's key intellectual property can be compromised and, as a consequence, affect pretax profits. The intellectual property in this case was customer trust. The beauty of this case is how we were able to help restore that customer trust.

I am always excited when I discuss the inheritance that exists within a business. In this situation, you will see that when the father ran the business, the company was number one in its market based on customer trust. No question! The sons inherited this legacy of customer trust but began to lose it. As I have mentioned before, future prosperity is found in the intellectual properties that make up the inheritance of a business. This case is a classic example of that principle.

Case 12

The Brothers Who Learned to Develop Trust

A father had passed the business he founded forty years ago to his two sons. This business created and printed marketing media for major American corporations. Culturally speaking, the two sons had been raised by their father to manage the business by jurisdiction. Each brother autonomously ran his own area of operations, but as the business grew, this fractured management resulted in a painstaking decision-making process. Worse yet, the brothers did not trust each other, which in turn led to a lack of trust among the salespeople and customers.

We were recommended to the company by their asset-based secured lender to help the sons return their business to profitability. When we initially began our engagement with the owners and senior management, it was clear that we could not be successful unless we cured this core weakness first, even before we could start applying the BMM process. It readily became apparent that an immediate management change would be necessary.

After evaluating the possibilities, I quickly determined that the company's senior operating/financial executive was the best candidate for CEO. Over several meetings with the brothers, I discussed their willingness to do things differently. I eventually advised each of them to abdicate their authority and give a CEO the final daily authority to run the business, make decisions, and conform to the action plan that we would develop for their business through applying the BMM process.

Finally they both agreed. After meeting with the prospective candidate several times to determine if he wanted the CEO position, we developed a specific job description delineating his responsibilities and compensation package, and he accepted the opportunity. Had he declined, we would have brought in a new candidate or interim CEO.

Once we prepared a BMM process for the business and completed and implemented an action plan based on it, the CEO and owners began to trust one another. This *internal trust* became a created intellectual property that we could now use to build the business and create new intellectual properties.

At the same time, it was vital to recreate customer trust—another valuable intellectual property—that had been lost by the squabbling brothers. Although the quality of work performed by the business was excellent, customer trust was lacking specifically with regard to timely delivery. The business had often missed promised completion dates. With each son running his own jurisdiction, no one was responsible for overall management of customer commitments/production planning. Consequently production planning to support timely delivery of products/services to the customers was not met.

Now that a CEO was in charge of overseeing the entire business, we could institute the necessary changes to assure that in the future customers could count on timely delivery of the goods and services promised. To accomplish this, we developed and implemented a production schedule matching the BMM process sales by month. Within only a few months, the business was consistently providing its customers with quality products and services on time.

Every business owner knows how difficult it is to create a customer. What this business learned was *once trust was established in the management team and management could be trusted to consistently make responsible decisions, customers could trust that their deliveries would be on time, so they increased their purchase orders significantly!* Because sales from existing customers increased, the business did not have to secure as many new customers as it had previously estimated. The business had regained its customers by earning their trust, which is the most important intellectual property of a business.

The value of customer trust as an intellectual property has now been revealed. Prior to us getting involved, the two sons had been increasing the volume of their business by bringing in new customers at reduced prices. In addition, the sons were basically competing with each other just to obtain incremental profits to sustain their business. The new customers had minor or negative marginal profit contributions and caused additional disruption to the demands of production planning that increased delivery delays to both the new and existing customers. This situation, in turn, continued to contribute to a lack of customer trust. It was an amazing paradox: Increased business reduced incremental profits and led to a decline of customer trust.

This is a prime example of what I meant earlier in the book when I described how trusted economic theories are today actually creating a *pattern* that leads to unsustainable profits. In this case, the *pattern* involved

- Break-even theory

- ➢ Cost-led pricing theory
- ➢ Incremental profit theory

By basing their business decisions on those theories, the business experienced these interrelated problems:

- ➢ Accelerated decline in production/service life cycles
- ➢ Selling more for less
- ➢ Decline in pretax income
- ➢ No return on shareholder equity sufficient for investment to build a business
- ➢ Decline/erosion of customer trust

Once the business replaced the *pattern* by implementing the BMM process, it began to build to prosper by *restoring customer satisfaction and creating customer trust*:

- ➢ Customer trust earns adequate customer marginal profit contributions for future investments.
- ➢ Future investments build upon and create new intellectual properties.
- ➢ Building on intellectual properties creates innovations.
- ➢ Innovations result in new, creative products/services.
- ➢ New creations create customer trust.

This case study is a classic example highlighting the result of selling more at lower prices. Don't you find it remarkable that a business in this situation can be transformed into such a success?

The Value of Protecting Your Intellectual Properties

One of my mantras is that every business should invest in technology. *I strongly believe that the most important position in your business today is the senior executive responsible for innovation.* Great news! In *Worth* magazine's April/May 2013 issue, Claire Willet, in "10 Questions for your Chief Innovation Officer," discloses the following: 2012 saw Fortune 500 companies rushing to hire Chief Innovation Officers, a job that did not even exist until recently. In response to a question about the need for such a position in a small company, Per-Kristian Halvorson, CIO of Intuit, argued that not the size or revenue of the company but the commitment to innovation determines the benefit.

This final case will reinforce your ability to see how the value of intellectual properties in your business can help you grow and prosper for future generations. The BMM process is designed to draw out the real value of these intellectual properties and build upon them to create sustainable pretax profits. You will see how the BMM process saved the research and development arm of this high-tech business and, most importantly, enabled the company to go from massive losses to sustained prosperity.

Case 13

The Owner Who Saw the Light

This business created state-of-the-art wafer technology. The wafers were then used to manufacture products requiring laser light technology. This client had a great management team. The owner was brilliant. His vision toward advancing laser light technology was on the cutting edge of the industry. The owner had a chief operating officer who was his confidant, and between them they were bringing innovation to the marketplace.

Due to extraordinary investment costs of engineering research, however, the company had millions of dollars in pretax losses. Its secured asset-based lender was deeply concerned about these costs/losses and asked the business owner to obtain an independent opinion regarding these continued losses.

The company's CPA firm was nearing the end of the audit for the company at that time and advised the owner to expect a qualified opinion because the business was not a going concern. When we started our engagement, both the lender and CPA firm had grave concerns that this business would become insolvent. The intellectual property at risk, therefore, was the research and development department that creates new technology. The lender and CPA firm viewed this critical function as a cost draining cash out of this business. The lender wanted this department shut down.

Both the owner and his COO embraced our engagement and were committed to implementing the BMM process. Early on, as we were determining the profit improvement goal, it became clear that the business could *not earn sufficient pretax profits fast enough to meet the capital investment necessary to bring its innovation to market.*

As we worked with the owner to prepare the BMM, the lender asked to meet with me. The owner was in default of various loan covenants. The lender was prepared to call the loan unless the owners submitted a satisfactory business building plan. The lender requested that the action plan we developed to return the business to profitability be submitted within thirty days. More critically, the lender demanded that the business's research and development operation be shut down immediately! These were the only terms the lender was willing to accept to enter into a ninety-day forbearance agreement with the owner.

This meant we had a mere thirty days to convince the lender to give us a ninety-day forbearance agreement to continue in business. The owner seriously questioned if we could accomplish such a feat. I assured the owner that the BMM process is designed to complete the work necessary within a maximum three-week period. So, in order of importance, we completed the previous twelve months' adjusted sales analysis.

With this in hand, we prepared a production plan for the next twelve months. This process provided the ultimate solution to saving this business. We found that the assembly process was terribly inefficient. Subassembly shortages caused incredible delays in shipping products to customers, plus there were quality issues with the workforce. Management revealed that it was testing a subcontractor for this subassembly production process. I told the executive vice president that he had two days to determine if he was willing to completely outsource the process of subassembly.

Two days later he agreed to negotiate a contract with this vendor to perform all of the subassembly requirements. Because the business owner did not have cash to buy the necessary inventory, the owner agreed to require the new vendor to buy the inventory. The vendor agreed to the owner's terms. Within that same week, the executive vice president of operations initiated the process to lay off approximately one hundred employees. This process continued for a month as the new vendor stepped up its production capability. *These labor reductions saved millions of dollars and enabled the business to return to a minimum pretax profit within a month.* Cash flow immediately improved due to the labor savings and the vendor's buying the inventory.

We knew that this alone would not satisfy the lender, however, so we applied the BMM process to review the research and development department to determine whether it should be shut down. We discovered that certain engineers were starting to invest their time in new innovations instead of completing already planned product innovations. We also created a PERT chart to schedule completion of planned products within the next six months. *This plan gave us the opportunity to save millions of dollars annually in costs that were not part of the company's current business plan.*

As a consequence, we were able to save the core of the research and development department. We overlaid engineers so that as engineers completed their work at the beginning of a project's process they could begin work on new projects. Prior to that, all of these phases had been redundant (duplicated), resulting in twice the number of engineers and management supervision needed.

Our business plan in this case had about 25 percent lower sales for the future twelve months when compared to the previous year. When we completed our plan, the pretax profit exceeded 10 percent of the adjusted net sales model. This was remarkable!

With all these cost cuts and changes in production, enough pretax profits and cash flow existed that we could start to make monthly principal payments to the lender. We met with the lender within three weeks of starting our engagement. Part of the BMM process is to create a business plan with supporting monthly financial statements for the future twelve months, including a statement of operations/pretax profit, balance sheet, and cash flow projection. Our business plan also incorporated all the capital requirements of the research and development operation needed over the next six months to sustain the next generation of laser technology. We discussed our business plan and these supporting projected financial statements with the lender. After seeing that we intended to make monthly principal payments, the lender agreed to a six-month forbearance agreement.

The beauty of this case history about a business developing the next generation of wafer technology is that a new creation has occurred. I am not referring to the wafer. I am talking about the new customer that has been created. This new customer has now become an intellectual property. And, yes, this intellectual property is now part of the business's inheritance. This is the best example of creating social value, where new customers are created in the marketplace and goods and services are exchanged. This is sowing and reaping at its best.

We will close this chapter with another perspective from Peter Drucker. He once said that if you want to know what a business is, you must start with its purpose, and there is only one valid purpose of a business—*to create a customer.*

INTELLECTUAL PROPERTIES VS. THE EIGHT ECONOMIC THEORIES

—SEVENTEEN—

The J. C. Penney Action Plan

Earlier I mentioned the crisis that Ron Johnson, then-CEO of J. C. Penney, was facing in February 2013 and said that I would revisit his situation at the end of the book. Now that you are a graduate of the BMM process, I thought we could collaborate on those action items we might suggest to help return J. C. Penney to sustained profitability.

By now you understand which of the eight economic theories have not worked for your business. You have found the *pattern*. You have also listed the most significant intellectual properties of your own business. You understand the inheritance, the intellectual values you have created. As you have read this book, you have been developing action items as commitments for change to be implemented to return your business to earning sustained pretax profits. You are no longer relying on economic theories but the intellectual properties of your business to build on for prosperity.

Now let us take your suggested action items for J. C. Penney and combine them with the ones I have determined. My action items and commitments for change probably started just like yours. My first step was to assess the intellectual properties of J. C. Penney prior to Johnson's assuming the CEO position in November 2011. I came up with eight:

1. Customer trust
2. Customer loyalty
3. Reliable customer service
4. Reasonably priced merchandise
5. Dependable seasonal sales programs giving customers excellent discounted prices
6. Great customer demographics in many areas of the United States
7. A multitude of great store locations
8. Many veteran management and supervision personnel who promoted customer service

You can clearly see eight intellectual properties for growth vs. eight economic theories that did not work for Johnson at J. C. Penney. I am sure you listed some of these same intellectual properties and may even have thought of others that I have not considered. That is why collaboration during the BMM process is so critical! Now, as I outline the commitments for change I would suggest to J. C. Penney, you can compare your own thoughts and action plan.

First I believe that Johnson should have gone back to his valuable customers and told them that he had made several mistakes. He should have listed the key mistakes and asked these customers to forgive him. I believe that J. C. Penney is still an institution that Americans can be proud of. James Cash Penney built a brand based upon customer service no differently than Tom Watson built at IBM. Penney developed channels of distribution to his customers and created a delivery system that provided reasonably priced, quality merchandise to his customers, supported by dependable customer service.

You may recall that when I was in college I worked for IBM. I learned then about the importance of channels of distribution. IBM had great products, but most importantly a part of its delivery system to customers included the best field engineers trained to support these customers as products were being delivered. Whether a Fortune 500 company, a critical government department, or J. C. Penney, all customers deserve to receive excellent service.

So here in order of priority are my other action items for Johnson's replacement to consider in order to lead J. C. Penney forward to earning sustained pretax profits:

- ➢ For each month of 2011 and 2012, sales by category of each market demographic (customer) should be determined by store.

- ➢ The marginal profit contribution of each major category should be determined by store. This includes allocating all advertising costs to the categories.
- ➢ The marginal profit contribution by each store should be determined.
- ➢ An inventory of all remaining customer service personnel should be made current.
- ➢ A human resource report of the strengths and weaknesses of these personnel should be compiled.
- ➢ A merchandise inventory per store should be compiled. This report should separate the merchandise by season after removing slow-moving merchandise.
- ➢ The company should return to price-led costing. Merchandise should be priced so that the stores earn adequate profits that will yield J. C. Penney a consolidated 10 percent pretax profit return on sales. Reductions in corporate general and administrative expenses may also need to be made to reach this goal of 10 percent pretax profit return on sales.
- ➢ The 2011 and 2012 sales history by volume/mix of demographics will provide the possible base-line for modeling store sales expectations. A store

profitability model can then identify possible stores to be closed.

- Superior customer service must be reinstated. The best customer service people should be relocated to profitable stores or stores where a plan to return to profitability is possible. Training, development, and promotion of customer service personnel need to be implemented again.
- Merchandise inventory needs to be reallocated to open stores. Merchandise has to be available as advertised.
- Seasonal sales discount programs should be reinstated and promoted.
- J. C. Penney should place additional promotional emphasis on selling American-made merchandise.

In suggesting these action items, I wish to reiterate that I believe the board of directors is equipped to help J. C. Penney build to prosper. After reading this book, you probably also believe that the eight economic theories—the *pattern*—have simply misled the management team at J. C. Penney into decisions that have led to the current losses. However, I believe it is not too late to save this great American company. I believe J. C. Penney can regain its customer trust and build to prosper!

SOWING AND REAPING

— EIGHTEEN —

The New Dawn

By the time you have reached this chapter, you have gone from fear to hope. You were in fear because your business was being marginalized. You had reached the stage at which you had no more solutions to return your business to profitability. You had relied upon certain economic theories to help make your business profitable but now understand that these economic theories have not been relevant for decades, and they alone have contributed to your business becoming marginalized.

However, you have optimism about your future. Why? At the beginning of this book, you were a student of the BMM process. Now you have graduated; you have become a teacher. You know that you have multiple tools to use and to rely upon to create solutions that will return your business to sustained pretax profits.

As we discussed in an earlier chapter, American farmers have faith as they sow, and ultimately they reap at the end of each season as they harvest. Their business inheritance is the soil to nourish their seed as well as the seeds that create their prosperity. *In your case, your business is the soil and the seed of your inheritance. Sustained pretax profits ensure your business will be prosperous for generations to come.*

In this final chapter, I want to share one more case that describes how we were able to help save the business inheritance for a client and, as a consequence, how the company is seeing the fulfillment of its promise.

Case 14

Owners' Inheritance

This business was more than fifty years old. The owner and family involved in it had accumulated a substantial investment in buildings and property over the years that were used to support their distribution business. They bought products, stored these products, and then delivered them to end-user customers. Their business had grown over time to attain annual sales exceeding hundreds of millions of dollars. The owners had expectations of a pretax profit return on investment of 3 percent.

In 2007, however, their customers had started to significantly reduce purchases from the business as the US economy started to suffer. As these sales declined, the business began to lose, pretax, millions of dollars on an annual basis. The business's lender had advised that the company would be required to pay off its loan because the company had not met covenants in the loan agreement due to sustained pretax losses. The two prospective lenders each contacted me and referred me to these business owners in the belief that the owners needed help to restore pretax profits before the owners would be qualified for a new loan.

I first called on this client at its headquarters in late summer 2009. I remember the day because it was late on a Friday afternoon and 90 degrees outside. After the receptionist introduced me to the owner, we went to the board of directors' conference room. There was no air conditioning that day.

We began to discuss their business, and they indicated that although the business was not profitable at that time, they had completed a new business plan for the next three years that demonstrated that the business would return to profitability starting March 2010. They said over the past fifty years that their business never had declining sales for more than eighteen consecutive months. Consequently their new business plan for 2010 had more than $20,000,000 of projected increased sales. The business owners said that they could not imagine why these new lenders wanted them to get help. They were quite confident that their business plan was conservative and attainable.

I responded by asking if they had met their previous business plan projections for any of the past four years. Well, you would have thought I'd dropped a bomb. The temperature in the room increased to 110 degrees. Their answer was "No." They then continued to describe the conditions that had caused them to miss the projections for each of the past four years.

The meeting was not going well in my view. Nonetheless I asked if they were interested in my helping them reduce the possibility of not performing to their business plan and briefly discussed our BMM process. The business owner who served as CEO then asked me if I had ever managed a business like his. If I had not already realized it at this point, I knew for certain that I was in trouble. In this situation, however, my pride kicked in. I told him that I did not have industry experience but I was quite confident that I could return his business to profitability!

That did it. The CEO said he did not want help from me and asked me to leave and then escorted me out the front door. This was now a really bad day because I had to call both lenders and tell them something. The question was, what? I have long abided by a rule that I will always protect my clients' privileged information, so I wasn't about to tell the lenders that this prospective client had kicked me out of his office and did not want any help from me.

Thank God for that rule. I realized that my pride had gotten in the way, and I spent the rest of the afternoon trying to settle down. Once I regained my composure, I called both lenders and disclosed that I had met with the owners, who were quite confident in their business plans and wanted the opportunity to present those plans to the lenders.

Those calls went well. Now I had to confront my pride and call the CEO to ask his forgiveness for my comments about managing his business profitably. I had his cell number, so I decided to call him later that evening. He took my call. I told him how sorry I was for my pride and arrogance. I told him that I had confidence that the BMM process could help him and his management team but that I was just a business advisor helping business owners apply this BMM methodology to their businesses, not someone trying to manage their businesses. His response was amazing. He immediately forgave me and admitted that it was difficult for him to be questioned in that way. He said that he would take my comments to heart and that it was possible we might meet again. Soon after, I learned that he did successfully get a new lender who would pay off his existing lender.

But the story wasn't over. A year later, I received a call from another lender who informed me that this same business owner was asking for a loan. It turned out that the business owner had agreed to loan covenants that he could not maintain with his current lender and would prefer yet *another* new lender. The prospective lender then told me that they had referred this business owner to me to help him return his business to profitability and I should be expecting the owner's call. I only said "Thank you" to this prospective lender.

Now I wondered what I should do when the owner didn't call. To my astonishment, he did call me, and this time asked for my help. He said that he believed he could trust me. He said he saw my weakness in my pride but was pleased that I could quickly ask for forgiveness. He told me that he wanted to get started in applying the BMM process to his business, so we completed our assignment and aided him in obtaining the new loan.

As it happens, he and his co-owner have a substantial estate and often call me for estate planning advice. Recently they called and said that they had decided to prepare to sell their business and enter into an agreement with a partner to develop the real estate on which their business was situated. They would give up a significant portion of the real estate value to the developer, which would free up some cash, plus there would be proceeds from selling the business. I asked the owners questions about their customers and discovered that many of their major customers were gradually moving their business to different locations over the next five years. I then asked them if I could conduct an analysis and get back to them. They agreed.

In this situation, the analysis I was to prepare was to evaluate the existing values—the intellectual properties—of the business. In my view, these intellectual properties were the soil and seeds of their business, the inheritance they had built.

When the time came to meet with the clients, I told them that the answers were to protect all the inheritances of their estate. I advised them not to sell their business and not to give up a significant portion of their real estate. I reviewed all their intellectual properties with them. I advised instead that they would need to move their headquarters within the next five years to be responsive to their major customers and minimize delivery costs. I pointed out that their customers were growing significantly and that their business would continue to prosper, thus sustaining and even increasing their pretax profits. These increased pretax profits would be sufficient to finance their real estate development, and when they eventually moved their business, they could start their own development. It was not necessary nor in their best long-term interest to give up a significant portion of their property or to sell the business.

The business owners accepted these proposals.

My purpose in telling you about this real-life business case is to encourage you to continue in faith and start to apply the BMM process to your business to build on the inheritance of your company and reap the prosperous rewards. The fruit of our labor to create new customers is, indeed, our purpose. Creating new customers will be accomplished by sustained pretax profits reinvested by you in your business for innovation. Your existing and new customers trust that you will innovate. *Build to Prosper* is your new manual for innovation. Your mindset is critical toward building inheritances for our future generations. You have built your business from your original "visions" and "dreams." Abraham Lincoln had a dream, a vision. On July 13, 1862, before the Emancipation Proclamation, Lincoln told his Secretaries, Seward and Welles, that he (Lincoln) had come to the conclusion that "we must free the slaves or be ourselves subdued." Yes, in conclusion, I encourage you to innovate and not face the possibility of becoming subdued.

I would be most interested in hearing about your success with your action plan because I believe that your success can help others. Then, truly, we are students and teachers for each other. I am so grateful to you for reading this book, and I look forward to hearing from you. You can reach me at www.BuildToProsperBook.com.

Acknowledgments

I would like to express my heartfelt gratitude to Milli Brown of Brown Books Publishing Group, who saw the potential of my book and challenged me to pursue the ideal instead of the merely satisfactory. Milli was determined that this book be nothing less than the best it could be; her tenacity made me sit up and pay attention, and her skill, insight, and considerable know-how have made my vision a reality. Nan, who followed in Milli's faith, was an excellent "enhancement" editor. Milli, thank you for setting me on the path to success even on the days I dug my heels in. You and your staff are an exceptional treasure of the publishing world.

About the Author

Cameron J. McConnell is the CIO, Chief Innovation Officer, of Build to Prosper, a division of MGLLC. Build to Prosper helps business owners earn sustained pretax profits to reinvest in innovation. Cam's book, *Build to Prosper: Secrets for Sustained Profitability* is his manual for innovation. McConnell pioneered the Business Modeling Methodology (BMM) process, a ten-step business analysis tool that has proved to be consistently successful in enabling business owners to ascertain the pattern of their problem and identify the core intellectual properties they have created that can provide the foundation for restoring prosperity. McConnell received his business management degree from USC Graduate School of Business.

McConnell's first job at IBM, starting in 1966, offered him a unique opportunity to manage and operate the midnight shift for the company's emergency parts distribution center in Los Angeles. IBM taught McConnell valuable lessons about how IBM created products and services and developed channels of distribution to deliver these products on time to trusting customers throughout the world.

McConnell continued to hone his business consulting skills into the late 1970s. He worked as a CPA for KPMG as an international banking specialist, providing audit, management consulting, and tax services to KPMG International Banking clients on the West Coast. During this time, he began to offer suggestions to some of the largest banks in the world on how to improve their profitability. He also served as an instructor for the Becker CPA Exam Review and upper division intermediate accounting course at California State University at Los Angeles. These teaching opportunities were instrumental in McConnell's creation of the BMM process.

Following his work with KMPG, United California Bank (subsequently bought by Wells Fargo) hired McConnell to oversee the audit of its international bank practice. UCB had just lost $55,000,000 in its Basel, Switzerland, operation. McConnell helped establish the necessary international banking controls for all of its overseas divisions to prevent future losses.

McConnell's high visibility in international banking prompted the CEO of Purex to recruit him to review the company's sixty nonrelated businesses throughout the world and advise him on how best to build these businesses. During this process, McConnell substantiated that the return on investment formula taught as an economic theory was not reliable and discovered that most of the sixty businesses were applying cost-led pricing methods to determine the selling prices to their customers. He formulated his BMM process at Purex to require the businesses to apply price-led costing to determine selling prices.

At this stage in the development of his BMM process, McConnell was promoted to CEO of Purex's aeromotive subsidiary, the largest aeromotive company in the world. The company had just recorded a substantial loss due to the oil embargo, and many customers had grounded their jumbo jet fleets. For the next three years, he worked with his management team to apply the BMM process, which returned the company to earning sustained pretax profits that were reinvested into innovation.

The Junior Chamber of Commerce of Los Angeles chose McConnell as an executive of the year for the business recovery he led at the aeromotive company.

After eleven years in the corporate world, McConnell had achieved such consistent success with the results of his BMM process that he decided to found his own consulting business and help owners. McConnell Group, LLC is often called in by major lending institutions around the country to help clients earn sufficient pretax profits to be reinvested in innovation. To learn more, visit www.BuildToProsperBook.com.

McConnell and his wife, Ginny, currently reside in southern California, where four of their married children live. They also have one married daughter living in England and a married son who lives in Kathmandu, Nepal. They are proud grandparents and great-grandparents. For several years, the McConnells have supported and worked with MountainChild (www.mountainchild.org), a global charity based in Nepal that works to provide clean drinking water, educate children to help reduce child labor, and provide medical outposts in remote mountain villages. MountainChild also rescues children from the sex trade industry.